LANGUAGE AND THINKING
IN HUMAN DEVELOPMENT

Psychology

Editor

GEORGE WESTBY

Professor of Psychology
University College of South Wales, Cardiff

LANGUAGE AND THINKING
IN HUMAN DEVELOPMENT

D. G. Boyle

Lecturer in Psychology in
the University of Aberdeen

HUTCHINSON UNIVERSITY LIBRARY

LONDON

HUTCHINSON CO (*Publishers*) LTD
3 Fitzroy Square, London W1

London Melbourne Sydney Auckland
Wellington Johannesburg Cape Town
and agencies throughout the world

First published 1971

C

838746.

*This book has been set in Times type, printed in Great Britain
on smooth wove paper by Anchor Press, and
bound by Wm. Brendon, both of Tiptree, Essex*

ISBN 0 09 109590 5 (cased)
0 09 109591 3 (paper)

TO MY WIFE

CONTENTS

ACKNOWLEDGEMENTS

My thanks are due and are gratefully extended to Professor George Westby, who first suggested that I write this book. In its preparation I have been greatly aided by discussions with my colleagues in the Psychology Department of Aberdeen University, particularly Gerard Rochford, but all views expressed in the text are, of course, my own. Finally I wish to thank my typist, Mrs L. Gray.

I am grateful to the following publishers for permission to reproduce passages or figures from the works named: Bell Telephone Laboratories for Shannon's illustrations of approximations to English words, from *A Mathematical Theory of Communication* (ch. 3). George Allen and Unwin Ltd. for illustrative problems from *Thinking: An Experimental and Social Study* by F. C. Bartlett (ch. 7). Humanities Press and Routledge and Kegan Paul for two figures from *A Source Book of Gestalt Psychology*, edited by W. D. Ellis (ch. 7). Manchester University Press for a number of passages from Kant's *Prolegomena*, edited by P. G. Lucas (ch. 13). Victor Gollancz Ltd for two passages from *Language, Truth and Logic* by A. J. Ayer (ch. 13). Litton Educational Publishing Co for a passage from *The Crisis in Psychiatry and Religion* by O. H. Mowrer (ch. 14).

D.G.B.

PREFACE

The past twenty years have seen a resurgence of interest on the part of psychologists in what used to be called 'the higher mental processes', with the difference that whilst the earlier workers were concerned with the power of reasoning, recent interest has centred upon the use of language. This renascence has brought forth a few notable textbooks and numerous collections of readings, covering topics as diverse as the Hopi view of reality and experiments involving feeding different streams of nonsense syllables into the two ears of laboratory subjects. Not unnaturally students are frequently confused by the scope of the material, and find it difficult to integrate within an accommodating framework. In Parts One and Two of this book I have attempted to develop a suitable framework; in Part Three I have sketched the philosophical background to the current controversies in this area. As so many original papers are now so readily available in the collections of readings already mentioned I have not thought it necessary to go into the details of all the topics touched upon; readers of this book will therefore not find a guide to the trees, though they may obtain a plan of the wood.

I should like to draw attention to two features of the style. In the first place I have in a number of cases treated the same material from different points of view in different chapters, in order to show the interconnections of the data. Secondly I have more than once made points briefly rather than at length, in the belief that a nod is as good as a wink, not only to the blind, but to the farsighted too.

January, 1971   D. G. BOYLE
Aberdeen University

PART ONE
Language and Imagery

I

THINKING AND SYMBOLISM

The term 'thinking' is used in many senses, e.g., 'I'm thinking about it' means 'I'm turning it over in my mind': 'Think hard' is a directive to make a concentrated mental effort: 'Who'd have thought it!' is an exclamation indicating surprise. When psychologists use a term, however, they like it to refer to behaviour of some sort, and the behaviour of choice in regard to thinking is usually problem-solving. By way of preliminary, then, we offer the following indirect definition of thinking. When an animal or human being – or speaking more generally an organism – is faced with a task that it cannot immediately solve, but which it solves after an interval, then provided that the interval has not been entirely filled with random activity we can say that the organism has displayed thinking. In other words, we infer, from behaviour of a particular sort, that something has gone on, and what has gone on we call 'thinking'.

Let us see what this definition implies. It does not make thinking synonymous with problem-solving, but rather with a sort of symbolic activity that makes problem-solving possible. Not everyone would be happy with this definition, as many people like to regard the ability to think as an exclusively human attribute. To a large extent they are justified, for the ability to plan on a large scale, or to produce works of art or scientific genius, implies the ability to think of an order so much greater than anything that animals can manage as to seem altogether different. We must remember, however, that very few human beings are capable of such intellectual endeavour, and that in the vast range of human capabilities we find some people unable to cope with even simple everyday problems of living. When we consider not just the intellectual peaks but the valleys too, we find it very difficult to draw a sharp line between animals and men in this regard.

Before surveying some relevant evidence we must introduce some important definitions. When two animals meet and begin to interact the behaviour of one indicates to the other the appropriate way to respond. The behaviour of the first animal is a *signal* to the other. A great deal of behaviour, verbal and otherwise, comprises signals: many of our verbal utterances are signals as they indicate to other people the ways in which we intend to behave or want them to respond. Thus if when confronted by a plate of meat I say 'Ah!' I am signalling my pleasure at the occasion. If, however, I wish to discuss with a friend the merits of various dishes, signals are not adequate; for this purpose I require a set of sounds that are not directly linked to events, and we call these *symbols*. Signals and symbols are collectively known as *signs*, following the work of Charles Morris (the study of signs is called *semiotics*).

Not all symbols are linguistic. Indeed, language is a very sophisticated form of symbolism used for 'discursive' purposes, as Langer puts it. If I wish to represent certain aspects of experience to myself for the purpose of speculating upon them, as when I daydream, I am using *representational* symbolism (Langer prefers the term 'presentational', but 'representational' expresses better the use to which such symbolism is put, which is the main concern here). Only man can use discursive symbolism, but it is quite likely that animals employ representational symbolism. There is, in fact, evidence from Yerkes and from Köhler that chimpanzees respond with irrational fears to the sight of certain objects, and take comfort from others: this strongly suggests that chimpanzees, at least, attach symbolical meaning to objects.

To summarise the previous two paragraphs we may represent the sign-using behaviour of organisms as follows, in which representation sophistication increases as we read downwards:

Signs: – signals

– symbols: – representational

– discursive

The ability to use symbols greatly facilitates learning, and particularly problem-solving. Let us now survey some animal behaviour in regard to learning and problem-solving to see if we can interpret any of it as exhibiting the use of symbols.

If we examine the ability to solve problems displayed by various types of animal, we find a steady progression as we ascend the phylogenetic scale. The first evidence of the ability to learn, i.e., to modify behaviour positively and relatively permanently on the basis of past experience, comes with worms, who have a nervous system with a simple brain. Without its brain the worm continues to live but cannot learn even a simple response such as turning in the correct direction at a junction in a maze in order to reach food. With its brain a worm can not only learn to turn left rather than right, but can alter its behaviour when the experimenter changes the food from the left arm to the right arm of the maze. With successive alternations of the postion of the food, the worm shows an increased facility at appropriately reversing its behaviour.

Insects show remarkably complex behaviour, the best-known example being the figure-of-eight dance performed by a scout bee on returning to the hive, to indicate to fellow workers the distance and direction of pollen (von Frisch[1]). However, the abilities of insects cannot be unequivocally interpreted in terms of learning, and much of their behaviour appears to be based on instinct, i.e., the inheritance of motor patterns. Insects seem, in some ways, to be an offshoot from the main stem of evolution, as if nature had developed an alternative mechanism to intelligence. Some people have claimed to have demonstrated that insects can learn, for instance that honey bees can be taught to discriminate colours, and that ants can learn to run mazes, but interpretation of evidence in this field is far from certain.

When we come to birds we find a rudimentary learning ability, consisting mainly of the ability to integrate the various movements involved in feeding. Nevertheless, simple discriminations and generalisations are possible: for instance, if hens are taught to peck at the darker of two patches of grey in order to obtain food, and the absolute values of the patches are changed, so that they are both lighter or darker than they were but one is still darker than the other, they will continue to peck at the darker patch.

The greatest ability to learn is displayed by mammals, and their ability in this respect is such as to suggest very strongly that they are capable of symbolic activity. At the simplest level we have the delayed reaction experiment. A hungry animal is shown food, which is then hidden under one of a number of boxes. After an interval the animal is allowed to approach the boxes for the food. The higher up the phylogenetic scale the animal is, the more successful it is at remembering which box hides the food. Dogs usually need to stay pointing at the correct box in order to solve the problem, but monkeys can remember even if they are turned around before being released. A more advanced task involves the 'temporal maze', in which an animal has repeatedly to go up a path between two obstacles, and

---

[1] When names of authors appear in brackets, they refer to works, by those authors, which are listed in the bibliography at the end of this book.

turn left or right in a sequence decided arbitrarily by the experimenter. Higher animals can solve this problem, albeit with difficulty.

Whilst the results of these experiments may be interpreted in ways that do not necessarily imply the attribution to animals of symbolic activity, there are other experiments that do seem to require this interpretation. One is the celebrated experiment by Krechevsky (later known as Krech), who showed that rats running mazes, in which the alleys were painted black or white, or were differentially illuminated in ways that bore no relation to the correct path, made systematic choices in accordance with these differential cues, as if they were testing 'hypotheses' about the maze. Another is the series of experiments by Wolfe and by Cowles, in which the investigators taught chimpanzees to work for poker chips which they could exchange for food from a coin-operated machine. Not only did the chimpanzees master the task, but some animals learnt not to exchange the poker chips immediately, but to accumulate a number of them. More recently Premack has taught a chimpanzee to associate plastic chips of various colours with different fruits, and to use the chips to 'request' fruit.

Evidence such as this supports the argument adduced earlier that it is difficult to draw a hard-and-fast line between animals and men in regard to problem-solving. It might be objected that human beings alone are capable of producing original solutions in response to problem situations, but even this is not true. Two experiments will illustrate the point.

First, Maier's reasoning test for rats. Fig. 1:1 illustrates the problem. The rat was allowed to explore the room, the ringstand 4 at the far left, and table *A*, reached by climbing the ringstand. After the rat was thoroughly familiar with the set-up, table *C* was added, along with the bridge leading to the food. Ringstand 4 was now removed. Ringstands 1, 2, and 3 now led to table *C*, and the rat was trained to climb one of these stands and reach the food by crossing to table *C* and then the further bridge to the food.

The rat now has learnt two patterns of behaviour. The first, which we may call Experience 1, is learning to run from any part of the room on to table *A*, via ringstand 4. The second, Experience 2, is climbing one of ringstands 1, 2, and 3, to reach the food by way of table *C*. If now the rat is placed on table *A* with ringstand 4 once more in position it must produce a new response in order to reach the food. It must descend ringstand 4, cross the room and ascend one of the other ringstands. This new response is a synthesis of Experiences 1 and 2. About 80 per cent of Maier's rats were able to do this (Maier, 1929).

A more celebrated investigation was made by Köhler with chimpanzees. A chimpanzee was placed in a cage and tethered to a tree, with a stick within its reach. A banana was placed outside the cage, outside the chimpanzee's unaided reach, but the animal eventually picked up the stick to use as an implement to draw in the fruit. In a further experiment the stick was too short, but the animal

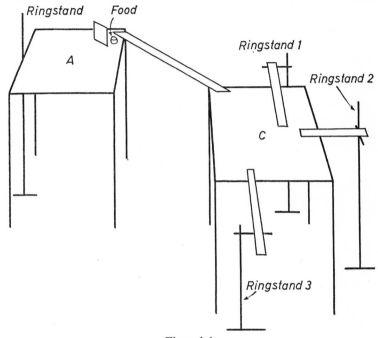

Figure 1:1
Maier's reasoning test for rats.

could use it to draw in a longer stick to use as an implement. Finally the situation was so arranged that two sticks had to be fitted together to make a longer stick in order to obtain the food. This was very difficult to solve, but one chimpanzee, after manipulating the sticks for some time in a futile manner, solved the problem quite suddenly. As a result of the animal's manipulations the sticks were aligned, and the animal behaved as if he 'saw' that they could be joined together. This was an integration of two aspects of experience into a new way of regarding things or, as it is usually called, 'insight'.[1]

[1] For a useful collection of readings on animal problem-solving see Riopelle.

It is difficult in the light of such evidence to argue that the problem-solving abilities of human beings involve a totally different set of abilities from those of animals. Certainly man's abilities are of a higher order, primarily because of his powers of symbolism expressed in written language and mathematics. Mathematical symbolism in particular enables us to make statements like the following:

$$(p+q)^n = p^n + np^{n-1}q + \frac{n(n-1)}{1x2}p^{n-2}q^2 \dots + q^n$$

Such statements appear to have nothing to do with reality, but have important applications in the real world.

At this point one might be tempted to categorise human thinking as thinking that employs discursive symbolism, and animal thinking as thinking employing representational symbolism. To do so would be an oversimplification as the following three problems make clear. In the first of the three, discursive symbols are employed in a deliberately misleading fashion. In the second and third the strong visual imagery aroused interferes with the exercise of discursive symbolism.

1. Three men in a restaurant are given a bill for £1–50. Each pays 50p. The waitress on reaching the cash desk realises that the bill should have been £1–30, so she returns 5p to each man and pockets the other 5p. Now each man has paid 45p. Three times 45p = £1–35. If we add the waitress's 5p we get £1–40. But we started with £1–50, so where is the missing 10p? People have been known to puzzle over this for hours before realising that the problem involves stating a meaningless equation, viz., £1–35 + 5p = £1–40; whereas the true equation is £1–35 − 5p = £1–30. Misstatement of the problem prevents the correct organisation of the elements needed for the solution.

2. Two jars A and B are filled respectively with pure water and pure whisky. A spoonful of B is added to A, which is throughly mixed. Then a spoonful from A is returned to B. Now is there more whisky in A than water in B, or vice versa, or are the amounts the same? The answer is the same, because the spoonful of A will contain a mixture of whisky and water, the amount of water in the spoon being equal to the amount of whisky left in the jar. The solution is prevented by the image of a small amount of whisky from B being diluted by the water in A (Wertheimer, 1945, 1959).

3. A rope is stretched tightly around the equator. One yard is added to its length. If it were rigid, how far would it stand off the earth (taking π as approximately 3)? The solution is simple. If the circumference of the earth is C and we add a length c to the rope, then

$$C + c = 2\pi(R + r)$$

where r is the increase in radius. Expanding and simplifying we find that $c=2\pi r$. We have been given that $c=36$ inches, so $r=6$. In other words the rope would stand 6 inches off the earth. People frequently refuse to accept the mathematical argument, because their image of the size of the earth will not accord with an increase of only one yard having this effect (Richmond).

Clearly a study of thinking will involve an examination of both language and imagery. We shall devote more time to language than to imagery, as language has engaged the attention of more psychologists than has imagery. Even so, the interest of psychologists in language is of fairly recent date (in the last twenty years or so) and much of our understanding of language comes from linguists and philosophers.

Language is, of course, used for many more purposes than to solve problems. In particular it is a far more effective means of communication than is available to non-human animals. Even so, much confusion can arise from the use and misuse of language. In this section we shall survey the development of linguistic ability in the individual, and examine its use in communication, before saying a little more about imagery. In the next section we shall examine the psychology of thinking in greater depth, then finally attempt to set the examination of language and thinking in the perspective of the philosophy and psychology of meaning, and of the higher mental processes in general.

2

THE DEVELOPMENT OF
LINGUISTIC COMPETENCE

There has been much dispute about the relationships of language and thinking, and there are two aspects to this dispute. On the one hand one may be concerned to know to what extent the possession of the discursive symbolism of language is a pre-requisite of the ability to think; this topic is discussed in Chapters 9 and 10. On the other hand one may wish to know whether the ability to *speak* is essential to thinking. J. B. Watson regarded thinking as 'subvocal talking', and experiments by Jacobsen, Max (1935, 1937), and Smith *et al.* adduced evidence to show that thinking is difficult, if not impossible, when muscular movements are inhibted. The notion that thinking is internalised speech can be traced back to Condillac's *Essai sur l'Origine des Connaissances Humaines* of 1746. Condillac proposed the idea to overcome a weakness in the formulations of Locke, in his *Essay on the Human Understanding* of 1690. Locke had proposed that we have ideas of sensation and of reflection, whereas Condillac wished to derive an account of thinking from one source only, namely sensation, and considered that the use of language to discuss sensations could account for what Locke had called ideas of reflection. The origin of the dispute was thus partly philosophical and partly psychological, as psychology had not been clearly distinguished from philosophy in the eighteenth century. Today, of course, the distinction is clearly drawn, but not all writers appear to be aware of the respective aspects of the problems they are discussing, a failure that leads to many futile disputes, particularly in the area of language and thinking.

Let us first discuss the development of language in children. In order to do this we must say something about how language is analysed, and the first distinction we must draw is between *phoneme* and *morpheme*. A phoneme is a sound that is recognised by native speakers to be a part of their speech distinct from other parts: thus in 'cat' we have three phonemes. There are three phonemes in 'cut', but the middle one is different from that in 'cat'. A native English speaker would easily recognise the difference, but the difference might not be so recognisable to a foreigner; to a foreign-born speaker the *a* in 'cat' and the *u* in 'cut' might sound like the same phoneme.

A baby is to some extent in the position of a foreigner in his own land, in that he has to recognise and produce phonemes if he is to establish effective communication with those around him. In the first year of his life he produces, spontaneously, nearly all the phonemes of all the world's languages (McCarthy). This stage is called 'babbling' and appears to be congenital, as even deaf babies babble. This activity appears to give the child pleasure, and children with normal hearing babble more, and for a longer time, than deaf children, which suggests that hearing their own vocalisations serves to reinforce vocalising.

Towards the end of the first year the baby attempts to imitate a vocalisation uttered by his mother or father. He succeeds in producing a meaningful speech sound, or morpheme. It has been suggested by Mowrer that the child tries to repeat sounds that he hears because he has heard them in pleasurable circumstances (e.g., being nursed), and he wants to recapture that pleasure. Only later does he learn to use words instrumentally, that is to get people to do things for him.

The ability of children to use language progresses rapidly as the child gets older. With regard to phoneme production, the ability to articulate depends upon the facial musculature and bone structure, the last sounds to be mastered being those made with the front of the mouth.[1] Consequently children may understand words that they cannot say. A similar phenomenon appears later when children may be able to point to an object named by an adult, though they cannot recall its name for themselves. This makes the assessment of children's vocabulary difficult, but all studies agree on its rapid development (3 words at one year, 270 words at two years; 1,500 at four years; 2,500 at six years, etc.).

One complicating factor in studying vocabulary is that a child's understanding of morphological rules, that is of how words are built up, enables the child to extend his vocabulary. If he knows that one forms a plural by adding -s, he can make 'cats' and 'dogs' from 'cat' and 'dog'. To demonstrate children's understanding of such rules one presents them with nonsense words like 'wug', and

[1] Speaking generally, consonants develop from back to front, vowels from front to back.

asks them to give the plural. Similarly one may ask them to write, from dictation, 'two nizzes', 'he nizzes', and 'a nizz's hat' (Berko, Berko and Brown).

One must distinguish a child's understanding of morphology from his understanding of syntactical rules, that is of the ways in which words are put together to form sentences. For instance, a French child learns that most adjectives follow the noun, whereas an English child learns that they precede it. How children master these rules is still a mystery, because they have a very good practical understanding by an astonishingly early age, usually before their sixth birthday.

A further complication in studying children's language development is that their powers of comprehension far exceed their powers of expression. Studies of the development of children's expressive ability show that the first attempts at linguistic communication (at about one year) are single words used to express a complete thought. These are called 'holophrases'. The thought expressed depends upon the intonation; thus 'Mama' can be a declaration ('There is Mother'); a demand ('I want mother'); an exclamation ('Fancy seeing Mother here!'); or an interrogation ('Is that Mother?'). This wide variety of usage makes many people suspect that intonation patterns are among the first linguistic elements to be learnt.

Towards the end of the second year the child progresses from holophrases to two-word sentences, in which one word is called a 'pivot class', the other an 'open class'. For instance, 'allgone' is a pivot in the following sentences: 'allgone jammy', 'allgone egg', 'allgone aunty'. Why the child progresses in this way from holophrases or how he goes on to master adult-type grammar by the age of six years is not understood. (The examples above are from Bruner, 1964. For a more detailed discussion see McNeill. Another useful summary is given by Carroll, 1960.)

Most words that the child learns he learns from the context in which he hears them. One way to investigate this phenomenon is to invent a synonym for a well-known word, then use it in sentences from which he has to deduce the word in question. For instance:

  1. A wet corplum does not burn.
  2. A corplum can be used for mixing paints.
  What is a corplum?

Here is another example.

  1. People talk about the bordicks of others but don't like to admit their own bordicks.
  2. People with bordicks are often unhappy.
  What does 'bordick' mean?

These studies (by Werner and Kaplan) are rather artificial, as the child is finding synonyms for nonsense words, whereas in real life he hears words and must learn what they refer to. He must distinguish the things referred to by a given term from things not so referred to; and must understand the reasons for the distinction. Thus he first learns that 'tree' is applied to some plants and not others; later he understands that a tree is a plant with a main woody stem reaching above a certain height. These properties constitute the *connotation* of 'tree'. The child can now apply the term to all plants with these properties, i.e., he understands the *denotation* of the term. When he can point to objects that he has never seen before, and say to what class they belong, he is said to have developed *concepts* (see Chapter 9).

Among the psychologists who have studied children's language is Piaget, who in 1924 distinguished between 'egocentric' and 'socialised' speech. Piaget claimed that most of the utterances of children under six years of age were references to themselves, and were not intended to be understood or responded to. The older child used his speech for purposes of communication, in particular for giving and receiving information. Independent investigators failed to confirm the high proportion of egocentricity in children's speech, but this failure may have been the result of a misunderstanding of Piaget's point of view. In a revision of his work, published in 1959, Piaget regretted that his use of the term 'egocentric' had misled some investigators into counting the number of times that 'I' or 'me' appeared in their speech. For Piaget egocentricity is defined in terms of the child's interpreting the significance of objects primarily with reference to himself, rather than to the wider context of which he later sees himself to be part. This can only be understood by sophisticated techniques of observation and questioning, such as have been developed by Piaget and his co-workers. (See Chapter 10 for further discussion of Piaget.)

There are two other schools of thought on this question – the Russian school, currently represented by Luria, which puts great emphasis on language as a factor in intellectual development, and the Harvard school, headed by Bruner, which, whilst not affording language the important role afforded to it by the Russians, nevertheless stresses its functional role as a tool for employing the intellect. (For further discussion see Chapter 9.)

Two points that this controversy suggests concern deaf children and bilingual children. With regard to the development of the intellect in deaf children, Furth adduces evidence to support Piaget's view of development. In other words, the intellectual development of deaf children may be slowed down, but follows the same pattern as that of children whose hearing is unimpaired. As for bilingual children there is some evidence of retardation compared to mono-lingual children, but it is likely that this is due to attempts to teach children by means of a language that they have not fully mastered, with resulting confusions (Haugen). It appears, therefore, that intellectual development, whilst intimately bound up in the normal individual with the development of language usage, does not simply reflect the development of linguistic competence.

Let us turn now to a consideration of attempts to explain the development of language usage by children. From learning theory the most fully developed account has been given by Skinner, in his *Verbal Behaviour*. Skinner's account of behaviour supposes that organisms spontaneously emit examples of behaviour, called 'operants'. In verbal behaviour these include names for things ('tacts') and requests ('mands'). Later they will include correctly structured sentences as opposed to incorrectly structured. The framework of a correct sentence is also treated by Skinner as a type of operant, known as *autoclitic*. If these operants are followed by reinforcement (which may be food, reduction of anxiety, or signs of pleasure on the part of the parent) they are repeated and hence strengthened. If not, they tend not to be used again.

This is probably a satisfactory account of the production of phonemes, for, as we have mentioned, the child spontaneously produces in his first year nearly all the phonemes in all the world's languages. By differential reinforcement the parents ensure that he retains the phonemes of his native language and no others. Even this is not entirely certain, because when he starts to use morphemes he is no longer producing independent phonemes, and morpheme production may represent a new form of learning distinct from the reinforcement of phonemes. However, when one turns to the under-standing and use of grammar, Skinner's account is far less satis-factory. For instance the notion of the framework of a sentence is notoriously difficult. The frame of the sentence 'John was hit by Bill' is: . . . was . . . by. Yet 'John was hit by accident', which appears to have the same framework, has a different *kind* of meaning, which one can only encompass in the theory by an *ad hoc* hypothesis such as that the framework of this kind of sentence is: . . . *was* . . . by *accident*, thus multiplying the number of autoclitics.

The chief criticism of Skinner comes from Chomsky (1959) who objects that Skinner uses terms derived from laboratory experiments as analogies in real-life situations. For instance, Skinner maintains that responses are under stimulus control, but as an example of stimulus control he gives the following instance: 'Such an expression as *A needle in a haystack* may be controlled as unit by a particular type of situation'. As Chomsky points out, to talk of 'control' here by analogy with the laboratory situation in which a hungry animal in a box presses a lever for food because the experimenter has arranged that this is the only way in which the animal will be fed is to make the analogy empty, and only speciously scientific. Similarly Skinner uses the terms 'response' and 'reinforcement' so loosely that they lack all objective meaning. A response in the laboratory situation can be precisely defined as a press on a bar, or a peck on the side of the box: to extend this notion to words, phrases, sentences, or exclamations is, once more, to use an analogy with no scientific justification.

The main objection to Skinner, however, concerns his view that verbal behaviour develops under the contingencies of reinforcement obtaining in the verbal community in which the child grows up. Aside from the general controversy as to whether reinforcement is always necessary for learning, which occupied much of the energies of Hull and Tolman (see Broadbent, 1961), there is the specific issue of whether the reinforcement conception adequately accounts for the known facts about language development. Chomsky declares quite definitely that it does not. He says: 'I have been able to find no support whatsoever for the doctrine of Skinner and others that slow and careful shaping of verbal behaviour through differential reinforcement is an absolute necessity. If reinforcement theory really requires the assumption that there be such meticulous care, it seems best to regard this simply as a *reductio ad absurdum* argument against this approach.'

Chomsky's own view of linguistic ability is that it develops independently. The speaker makes his own contribution, which he does not have to learn from others. This is an embarrassment to learning theory, which is the motivation for Skinner's attempt to account for the use of language solely in terms of external shaping; as Chomsky says: 'Elimination of the speaker and learner . . . can be achieved only at the cost of eliminating all significance from the descriptive system, which then operates at a level so gross and crude that no answers are suggested to the most elementary questions.'

The questions that must be answered, in Chomsky's opinion, concern the internalisation of grammatical rules that permit us immediately to recognise whether a sentence, which we have heard for the first time, is or is not legitimate in terms of the grammar of our native language: and which permits us to utter grammatically correct sentences that we have never before uttered or heard uttered by others. The fact that children acquire these abilities at a very early age suggests to Chomsky that human beings are somehow innately 'designed' to do this.

We shall take up Chomsky's views again in Chapter 4, but we must indicate here that Chomsky has not been without his critics. Both Broadbent (1970) and MacCorquodale have come to the defence of the behaviourist approach to language. In essence the dispute is methodological: if one believes that behaviourism is a valuable approach to psychological problems, then it is both legitimate and necessary to seek to demonstrate that language can be discussed in behaviouristic terms. If, like Chomsky, one does not, one can all too easily spot the terminological attenuations that pass for rigorous concepts. The question is whether to strengthen the conceptual framework or to reject the approach altogether. The alternative one chooses will depend upon one's methodological predilections. (For discussion of another behaviouristic approach see Chapter 12.)

One weakness of Chomsky's approach is the suggestion that linguistic ability may be innate. To suggest that any human ability may be innate makes many psychologists uneasy, despite the evidence from ethologists (e.g. Thorpe) that much animal behaviour has an innate basis (the role of instinct in human behaviour has been discussed by Fletcher). MacCorquodale points out that, even if there is an innate component in language, one still needs hypotheses about learning to account for the form that language takes. Both MacCorquodale and Broadbent have argued that much of the apparently fantastic ability of children to handle grammar at an early age has its analogy in the ability to generalise displayed by rats in the experimental laboratory.

The possibility that language development is instinctive is an old one, and was discussed by Langer some years before the Skinner/ Chomsky debate. Langer points out that children who do not grow up in language communities probably do not acquire language, although the evidence on this point is from unsatisfactory sources such as Itard and Gesell on wolf children.[1] The important facet of human behaviour in Langer's view is the ability to make re-presentational symbolisations of the universe. This ability, allied to the speech play of the young child, is probably the origin of language. If this view is correct, then both Chomsky and Skinner are partially right, but it is unlikely that either has expressed the whole truth.

---

[1] See Lenneberg's view in Chapter 13.

3

COMMUNICATION

The heading of 'communication' covers so many topics as to make it virtually impossible to make a coherent whole out of them. This chapter will not, therefore, attempt to summarise the acoustical, physiological, and engineering aspects of the subject. Instead it will look at various linguistic topics from a psychological point of view, to see to what extent they contribute to solving our central problem.

We shall start by making the suggestion that communication, for a psychologist, involves meaning and intent. This is by way of being an indirect definition of communication, and like all definitions it is inherently unsatisfactory. For instance, when my cat rubs against my legs then walks to her empty saucer, I understand her to mean that she wants some more food; and I see no good reason to deny that she intends me to understand her so. Yet when a worker bee performs a figure of eight dance at the entrance to a hive, I find it difficult to imagine that the bee *intends* to communicate to fellow workers a message about the distance and direction of pollen. That may be the meaning of the dance to an observer, but it is doubtful whether the bees are capable of this type of understanding. However, disputes about the precise point on the phylogenetic scale at which conscious awareness appears are sterile at worst and trivial at best: since in any case the present concern is primarily with human communication, we shall rest content with our heuristic definition of communication as the intentional transmission of a meaningful message.

What makes human communication so much more efficient than that of other animals is, of course, the possession of language. We must, therefore, examine language as a means of communication. Much attention has been paid in recent years to the discipline called 'information theory'. Unfortunately this discipline studies the transmission of information irrespective of the sense of what is conveyed. It is therefore of limited relevance to psychologists interested in meaning. Nevertheless we do transmit sounds, which other people receive by way of their sense organs; if the receptor mechanisms are faulty, or if the transmitted message is distorted on its way to the receiver, the intended meaning will inevitably be affected. Thus we must briefly summarise some of the main points at issue.

In information theory, we have said, communication is the transmission of information. If we imagine a sack of billiard balls, on each of which is a letter, with some billiard balls having the same letter as others, then we can write a mathematical equation describing the amount of information we should obtain by drawing out billiard balls at random. If the total number of billiard balls $=n$, and the number of different letters $=a$, then the quantity of information (I) is given by $I = k \log a^n$.

In fact this situation never obtains in the case of verbal communication. The reason why it does not is that all channels of communication are liable to interfere with the transmission of a message. This effect was first studied with respect to telephones, where extraneous noises such as crackling and buzzing may interfere with the transmission of a message. Consequently the term 'noise' has come to be used for anything that interferes with a channel's powers of transmitting information.

How do we overcome the effects of noise? We do this by introducing redundancy, that is, by saying more than the minimum. We can do this either by repeating ourselves or by saying the same thing in different ways. Another way of introducing redundancy is to make rules such as 'u always follows q' or 'i before e except after c', so that we can spot a mistake when it occurs.

The effect of introducing redundancy by making rules is to make certain sequences of letters and words more likely than others. Suppose that we were constructing a language of three letter 'words' from the symbols 0 and 1, we could make 8 words, viz., 000, 001, 010, 011, 100, 101, 110, 111. Let us suppose that we were sending a message with these words, we should be likely to make mistakes, because only one error would change, say, 000 into 001, or 101 into 011.

The way to overcome this difficulty is to select only certain 'words' for our language, say: 011, 110, 000, 101. Now it would take *two* errors to transform any one of these into any other: if only one error had occurred (for example, if we had received 001) we should know immediately that there had been an error.

What we have done here is to use only four words out of our possible eight. In order to transmit the same amount of information as before, we must repeat our words, and we shall probably have to employ the words in different combinations. Thus we have introduced redundancy, at the same time as reducing the possibility of error: we have done this by reducing the amount of information that can, in theory, be transmitted by the symbols in our set.

Most languages are highly redundant, that is, the number of combinations of letters and words used in practice is considerably less than would be possible in theory, because languages have built-in rules that make certain combinations impossible. Two of these rules (for English) we have given already: the effect of these rules is to make us spot immediately if an error has been made in certain cases, e.g., 'qn' is obviously a mistake for 'qu'.

The trouble with redundancy is that it occasionally makes for awkwardness of expression. The sentence 'John walked to the door, picked up John's coat and John's hat and put on the coat and the hat' is very cumbersome. In practice we should say 'John walked to the door, picked up his hat and coat, and put them on'. We use pronouns, which are a little ambiguous, in order to facilitate expression. We have, in fact, *reduced* redundancy because the probability of making an error here is very small. It is obvious from the context what the pronouns 'his' and 'their' refer to. This is not always so, and ambiguities may lead to misunderstanding.

Before leaving the topic of noise in the transmission of messages we must note that the human ear has a remarkable capacity for ignoring irrelevant material when receiving messages, and can understand speech even when it is subjected to very considerable distortions. Cherry among others has investigated the effect of playing irrelevant material by tape to one ear whilst requiring the subject to follow a message fed to the other ear, and Broadbent (1958) has proposed a filter model to account for the selection of some material and the exclusion of other. The question as to the level of the organism at which this filter operates is a point of current controversy in the psychology of attention (see Treisman for an illustrative paper on the topic).

We have mentioned the effect of context in clarifying meaning. The word 'context' is a little ambiguous; it may refer to the fact that we put things in writing in a way that we do not adopt when talking or to the fact that we talk differently to adults and to schoolchildren. There is, however, another meaning. Whatever the audience or the mode of communication the word 'the' is more likely to be followed by a noun, an adjective, or an adverb, than a pronoun or another article. Similarly an adjective is more likely to be followed by a noun than by any other part of speech. In these cases, what one says will be affected by what he has just said, and also by what he intends to say. In these cases we talk of the effect of 'verbal context'. The 'verbal context' of any utterance is made up of the utterances surrounding it.

Previously we were talking of the probabilities of occurrence of certain sequences. We observed that sequences of words are necessary for the transmission of messages, and we know that languages have rules that say whether an adjective comes before or after a noun, or what types of word may follow an article and so on. Consequently these rules, by determining the likelihood of one word following another, help to define the verbal context. Let us see how.

A man knowing no English, who wanted to write English essays, might draw words at random from a dictionary. His sequence would be a *zero-order approximation to English*. The same man, given statistical information about the relative frequencies of communication units, might draw words so as to correspond to these frequencies. He would have a *first-order approximation to English*.

Given a list of pairs of words, he could choose one pair, e.g., 'goes down', look at all pairs beginning with 'down', and choose, perhaps, 'down to', and so proceed. He would now have a *second-order approximation to English*, e.g., 'do go away from cheese biscuits taste tongue tied tightly shut tight fisted workman ambidextrously able seaman sails away from Russia'. Given a list of triplets, e.g., 'she was bent', he would choose one triplet, then look at all possible triplets beginning with 'was bent' and perhaps choose 'was bent and', and so proceed. He would have a *third-order approximation*, e.g., 'drink up fast against the wall is high up on to the abattoir was dirty old devil Mephistopheles dies unhappily because of love and kisses fail'. Words grouped in fours would yield *fourth-order approximation*, e.g., 'take no notice of the abatement there upon the sofa lay upsidedown thoughtfully contemplating infinity while munching meticulously slowly and cautiously otherwise the moral code of love affairs had gone far'. It would be possible to punctuate this to obtain fairly plausible sentences, e.g., 'Take no notice of the abatement. There upon the sofa lay upsidedown, thoughtfully contemplating infinity, while munching meticulously, slowly, and cautiously. The moral code of love affairs had gone far.' We have had to omit only one word – 'otherwise'.

In a rather similar way we can imagine how words may be constructed. By drawing at random the letters of the alphabet plus a space, we have a zero-order approximation to words, e.g.:

xfoml rxklrjffuj zlpwcfekscy fteyckcqsgxydahnbix

(This and the following examples are from Shannon.) This does not look much like a language, but if we draw letters and spaces according to their frequency of occurrence, thus obtaining a first-order approximation, we obtain something that looks like a language, albeit not English, e.g.:

tocro hli rgwr nmilewis eu ll nbnesebye thl eeits

Here is an example of a second-order approximation, obtained by drawing each letter according to the likelihood of its following the preceding one.

on ei antsoutinys are t infore st b s deamy thall

A third-order approximation is one in which each letter is drawn according to the probability of its following the previous two. Here is an example:

in no ist lat why cratict froure birs grocid pondenome of demonstures of the reptagin is regoactiona of cre

The conclusion of these examples is that the greater the amount of context determining each unit, the more familiar is the appearance of the resulting sequences of words and letters (Miller, 1951; Miller and Selfridge).

One interesting feature of approximations to sentences that sound almost like intelligible speech but not quite is their resemblance to the speech of schizophrenics. The resemblance may be no more than superficial, but a major characteristic of schizophrenic speech is that the listener feels that he has almost understood but not quite. It is as if the sequences of words used by schizophrenics are not determined by the same statistical rules of context as govern normal speech (see also Chapter 5).

So far we have been examining some studies that shed light on the understanding of the content of messages. We must now look at the structure of the messages themselves. If spoken utterances are to convey meaning they must first be understood by the person hearing them. Therefore both speaker and hearer must have an agreed framework of speech sounds. They must also agree on the order in which utterances are put together. The speech sounds may be studied by the techniques of phonetics and phonemics (phonetics being a system of classifying speech sounds, phonemics a method of describing these sounds in terms of how they are produced – see Cherry for details of phonemics). Early linguists were much concerned with phonemes and morphemes: only more recently have they been concerned with syntactics, i.e., a study of meaningful word order. To oversimplify the picture considerably, we may say that there are two main schools studying linguistic structure: the Continental school, concerned with the structure of utterances, and the American school, whose best-known member is Chomsky, concerned with 'transformational-generative grammar', which is of particular interest to psychologists. We shall give an account of Chomsky's views later. First, though, we must say something about phonemes.

A phoneme is a kind of average speech sound. A thousand native-born English speakers may pronounce the *u* sound in 'cup' with many different shades of difference in pronunciation. As long as they all recognise the sound and its difference from, say, the *a* in 'cap', we can regard the sound as a phoneme in their speech.

In spoken English there are 44 sounds (phonemes) made up as follows: 12 vowels, 9 diphthongs, 23 consonants. There are, of course, 26 letters of the alphabet. Of these, *q*, *c*, and *x* are superfluous, as *k* and *ks* make the sounds represented by *q*, *c*, and *x*: so, as far as the possibility of representing sounds is concerned, there are effectively 23 letters of the alphabet. Some people go further and argue that *j* does not represent a phoneme, but a combination of the phonemes *dg* as in 'judge', which would reduce the effective number of letters to 22. Thus the number of letters is exactly half the number of phonemes that they are required to represent, which leads to ambiguities in the pronunciation of written language, and contributes to reading difficulties (see Carroll, Cherry, Miller (1951) and Potter).

In spoken language such difficulties do not arise, particularly as 9 phonemes make up more than half our vocal utterances. They are *i* (as in 'bid'), *n*, *t*, *r*, *e* (as in the indeterminate 'the'), *s*, *d*, *a* (as in 'bad'), and *l*. (One interesting feature of these phonemes is that most are made with the lips and tip of the tongue, i.e., they are among the last to be learnt.) The fact that most of what we say is made up of 9 phonemes indicates that there is a great deal of redundancy in our verbal behaviour. We shall encounter redundancy again in connection with Basic English (Chapter 4), which is made possible by the fact that much of what we have to say can be expressed by fewer than 900 words out of the half-million or more available to us. Redundancy appears to be a pervasive feature of verbal behaviour, as most of our speech is made up of 70 syllables, mostly monosyllables, the commonest being the indeterminate 'the'.

Another aspect of redundancy in language usage was noted by Zipf, in his wide-ranging search for the 'principle of least effort'. He observed that some words are used more frequently than others, and

educed a relationship between number and frequency. Let us suppose
that we discover that 300 words in a passage are used 3 times,
200 words are used 4 times, 60 words, 7 times, and 30 are used
10 times. If we multiply the numbers of words (n) by their frequencies
(f) we obtain nf, with the following values:

$$
\begin{aligned}
300 \times 3 &= 900 \\
200 \times 4 &= 800 \\
60 \times 7 &= 420 \\
30 \times 10 &= 300
\end{aligned}
$$

There is no clear relation here, but if we had multiplied n by f^2
instead of f, we should have obtained the following values:

$$
\begin{aligned}
300 \times 9 &= 2700 \\
200 \times 16 &= 3200 \\
60 \times 49 &= 2940 \\
30 \times 100 &= 3000
\end{aligned}
$$

The values of nf^2 are all of the same order. Zipf formulated this as a
law, $nf^2 = K$. The law breaks down for articles, because 'the' and 'a'
will be used so frequently that the value of nf^2 will be very high.
Nevertheless, for most words the law holds approximately true.
(See Cherry, Miller 1951, for further discussion of the statistical
approach to language.)

Let us now turn to a discussion of the work of the American
linguists on syntax. This work has been concerned with formulating
a grammar, or the rules for constructing a grammar. The grammar
must satisfy certain criteria, of which the following is of especial
importance: the sentences that the grammar generates will be acceptable to a native speaker of the language. Any grammar that
permits the construction of such sentences as 'I left for the hour at an
early country' will clearly be inadequate, because the word order
is unacceptable. Chomsky and some other American linguists want
to construct a grammar that permits the formulation of syntactically
correct sentences without reference to the meaning of these sentences
(Chomsky 1957). To illustrate the independence of syntax and sense
Chomsky gives the sentence: 'Colourless green ideas sleep furiously',
which every native-born English speaker will recognise as perfectly
grammatical although quite meaningless. Whether or not meaning
can be so readily divorced from grammatical structure except in
extreme instances is a point of controversy, but it is a controversy in
linguistics rather than in psychology, so it need not detain us.
Briefly, Chomsky argues that no one has yet shown that it is possible
to construct an adequate grammar even *with* knowledge of meaning,

so from a grammatical point of view meaning is irrelevant. This exclusion of meaning may seem to make syntactics, like information theory, of limited relevance to psychology but, whilst word order may not be determined by meaning, meaning is to a very great extent dependent upon word order, so the work of Chomsky and others is of considerable interest to psychologists.

One reason for their interest is the assumption by Chomsky and his co-workers of an innate ability in human beings to understand the structure of language, so that a child can infer, from what he hears his parents say, how to construct sentences himself. He learns how to generate new sentences himself, and to understand such transformations as from active to passive voice. Hence the term 'transformational-generative grammar'.

We can give here only an indication of this approach, remembering both that the approach is controversial, and that the controversy is properly one for the linguists. Consider the sentence 'This dog bit that man'. This can be regarded as made up of a noun phrase ('the dog') and a verb phrase ('bit that man'). The noun 'dog' has a determiner 'this': the verb phrase contains a verb ('bit') and a further noun phrase ('that man') made up of a determiner '(that)' and a noun ('man'). The verb stem is 'bit', but the verb is in the past tense, a fact that we can regard as auxiliary information. We can thus lay out the structure of the sentence as in Fig. 3:1. This type of analysis may be applied to all sentences, and illustrates their underlying structure.

More important is the attempt to specify rules for transformations, to explain how it is that we understand that 'the dog bit the man' (active) means the same as 'the man was bitten by the dog' (passive). In terms of the analysis given above, we may write 'the dog bit the man' as $Det + N_1 + Aux + Vs + Det + N_2$, or simply as $NP_1 + Aux + Vs + NP_2$. We may write 'the man was bitten by the dog' as: $NP_2 + Aux + be + en + Vs + by + NP_1$. This analysis shows that the noun phrases change places, the auxiliary stays the same i.e., the past 'bit' is matched by the past 'was', but we have some form of the verb 'to be', and we have a past participle as represented by *en*. We also insert *by* before the final noun phrase. Applying this analysis as a rule, we can generate any number of passive transformations from the active voice. (For further discussion see Bolinger, ch. 12, and Herriott.)

Impressive though this analysis is it may leave the reader with the impression that it has explained nothing about the child's ability to master the complexities of grammar, but has made amply clear what those complexities are. To suggest that the ability to communicate through the medium of language is innate is no explanation at all: rather it relegates linguistic communication to the realm of un-explainable facts. We shall take up this point again in later chapters.

Let us now try to draw together some of the disparate threads of this chapter. We began by suggesting that communication involves meaning and intent. The topic of meaning is a very important one for psychology, and one that exists on two levels. At one level the psychologist must attempt to make sense of what organisms do, which is to say that he must find some meaning in what they do. At

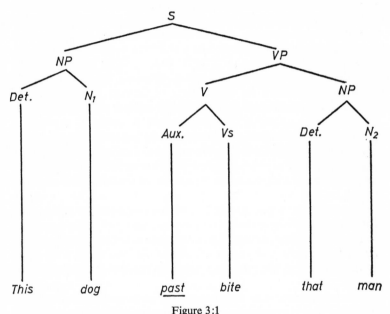

Figure 3:1
The deep structure of a sentence.

the other level he will, if he is wise, acknowledge that organisms make sense of their experiences, and he must attempt to discover what that sense is. Unfortunately psychology has turned its back on this task because, since a psychologist's hypotheses about an animal's experience cannot be confirmed, psychologists have to a large extent ceased trying to understand other human beings as well. Psychology will probably not progress out of its behaviouristic impasse until it makes the study of meaning its central concern.

The view proposed here is that the chief intellectual task of the individual is to make sense of the world that he experiences, and of himself as part of the world. This is not an original idea, but has seemed self-evident to many thinkers, the latest to give expression to it in psychological terms being Kelly. It is further proposed that, to the extent that the individual succeeds in this task, he can function in the world. Inasmuch as people grow up in communities it is not surprising that they make sense of the world in the same way (we shall defer to Chapter 14 a discussion of the possibility that it is an essential feature of human nature to make sense of the world in one way rather than another). Language is a uniquely human tool for making sense of the experienced universe.

It must be clear from what has been said in this chapter that meaning is not in a one to one relationship with sentences, as a meaning can be expressed in many different ways. Once more we encounter the phenomenon of redundancy, which appears to be a fundamental feature of human communication. The same phenomenon is encountered in other areas of human psychology. For example, the number of neurons in the central nervous system is enormously in excess of the number that is normally needed. In perception we encounter redundancy in the general phenomenon of constancy: we experience a stable universe of objects retaining their sizes, shapes and colours, despite enormous variation in the sensory information affecting our sense organs. From the mass of information we select that which makes a meaningful universe: and from the large number of linguistic elements at our command we select a few for purposes of communication. The two aspects of redundancy are, in the present view, closely linked, because it is proposed that *I can only communicate with you to the degree that you and I make sense of the universe in the same way, and express that sense in the same terms.*

Let us examine the implications of this proposal. The word 'meaning' has many senses, of which two are particularly important in the present regard. What I 'mean' by a sentence reflects both the sense that I make of the universe, and my attempt to display that sense to someone else. I may be relatively unsuccessful on both counts, and my hearer may diminish my chances of success still further by mishearing and/or misinterpreting what I say. Communication in such circumstances is probabilistic (compare Brunswik's view of the probabilistic nature of perception) although in most circumstances the probability of accurate communication is high: to draw another analogy with perception, we can say that most communication, like most perception, is veridical, that is to say that just as we see most things as they really are, so we usually understand other people accurately. Ambiguities are few when we discuss well-understood topics in simple language; but when we discourse of abstruse topics in complex ways we are likely to misunderstand each other. The view proposed here (which was italicised in the preceding paragraph) is that, for most practical purposes, we employ our language to confirm that the people to whom we are talking share our view of the universe.

It may be thought that this view is a reversion to a Cartesian solipsism, but the reverse is true. To the extent that we have grown up sharing a common view of the universe and learning to talk about it in the same way, we can communicate efficiently. It would seem to be an appropriate task for psychologists to investigate this common view of the universe, but few have done so. The most whole-hearted attempt to deal with man's intellectual grasp of the world is to be found in the work of Piaget. In their book *Mathematical Epistemology and Psychology* Beth and Piaget define the 'epistemic subject' as 'that which is common to all subjects at the same level of development, whose cognitive structures derive from the most general mechanisms of the co-ordination of actions' (p. 308). This concept, whilst not identical with our notion of common interpretations of the experienced universe, shares with it the assumption that the human intellect is capable of transforming the world of experience into coherent sense, and supports our view that communication is possible because intellects, though individual (in Piaget's terms the epistemic subject must be distinguished from the 'psychological subject'), share the power of representing the universe in a meaningful way, and displaying their representations to others. (See Chapter 10 for further discussion of Piaget's work.)

Most studies of communication are one-sided, in that they concentrate on the display aspect to the neglect of the representational. Such onesidedness is proper for linguists and communications engineers, but not for psychologists. The study of human beings' representations of the universe may not, however, be a task that psychologists can undertake alone. It may be a field in which psychologists and philosophers may work fruitfully together. (Further aspects of the problem of meaning are discussed in Chapter 11.)

4

CULTURE AND CONFUSION

Oscar Wilde's aphorism that Britain and America were two countries divided by a common language illustrates a longstanding awareness of the divisive influence of linguistic misunderstandings. Philosophers from the time of Descartes have urged the construction of artificial languages that would permit the absence of ambiguity in philosophical argument that characterises mathematics. One of the most celebrated of these philosophers was Leibnitz. However, the first successful attempt to construct an artificial language was made by an obscure Aberdeen schoolmaster named George Dalgarno who, in his *Ars Signorum* of 1661, described a *catalanguage* permitting precise reference to all parts of knowledge. The principle was that every major division of knowledge should be represented by a consonant, subdivisions by vowels, sub-subdivisions by consonants and so on, using consonants and vowels alternately, so that everything known could be named by a pronounceable polysyllable. In this way related objects would have similar names. Thus 'elephant' was *Nuka*, 'horse' was *Nuku*, 'donkey' was *Nuke*, and 'mule' *Nuko*. The idea was to name not only objects, but all 'notions'. This idea was promising, but inevitably limited by the extent of knowledge of the day; moreover much more flexibility is given by numbers than by letters, a fact recognised by library classification systems.

Towards the end of the nineteenth century there was great interest in the possibility of constructing artificial languages, to reduce international misunderstanding and promote world peace. The first of these was Volapük, but the most celebrated was, and is, Esperanto. Others included Ido, Esperantido, Novial, and Interlingua. The last, which was an attempt to modernise Latin so that every moderately educated person could understand it at sight, was constructed by Peano the mathematician, who was influenced by the work of Leibnitz. All these artificial languages suffered from various unsatisfactory features, including sounds pronounceable with ease only by Europeans, and the retention of grammatical superfluities.

Earlier in the present century there was a reaction against artificial languages, and scholars argued that less effort was required to master the English tongue to the extent of making oneself understood than to learn an artificial tongue. Whilst there are half a million word units in the *Oxford English Dictionary*, one can make himself understood by knowing only about 800. This fact was recognised by C. K. Ogden, who in 1934 constructed Basic English of 850 words, made up as follows: 600 nouns, 150 adjectives, and 100 other words such as verbs, pronouns, articles and conjunctions. This restricted vocabulary makes for circumlocutions, e.g., 'to walk' must be rendered 'to go on foot'. Furthermore such restrictions make it difficult to write creative literature, particularly poetry. This, however, is not a valid condemnation of an artificial language, whose function is to facilitate communication across natural language barriers. The languages mentioned above, and others, are discussed by Bodmer (ch. 11).

The ways in which the use of language can affect thinking was the concern of the group of linguists and philosophers known as the 'general semanticists' in the 1930s. Their idea was that in using words to describe experience we restrict the flexibility of thought, so philosophers must display the logical structure of language. The philosopher most closely associated with the philosophy of language was Carnap, but better known outside academic circles is the name of Benjamin Lee Whorf, the linguist. From his studies of the language of the Hopi Indians Whorf concluded that our very experience of the world is determined by the terms in which it is discussed by the language community in which we grow up. (This view was at one time shared by Edward Sapir, and was known as the 'Whorf-Sapir hypothesis' although Sapir later changed his views – see Spier *et al.*) Thus the logical categories described by Kant as the intuitive framework of thought (such as space, time, motion, causality) are not universal in human nature, but only seem so because it is in such terms that Indo-European languages describe the world.

One important difference between the Hopi language and ours is in terms of time. We speak of time as if it were extended analogously with space: the Hopi talk rather of intensity. Thus if I strike a table three times I say that I have been striking the table for longer than if I had struck only twice: the Hopi would express the difference by saying that three blows is greater than two blows. Another difference concerns nouns and verbs. Lightning for us is a brief event, and hence referred to by a noun, whereas for the Hopi it is a verb. This may seem strange, but we use 'rain' as a noun in the sentence 'the rain falls', yet in the sentence, 'it's raining' it would be inappropriate to ask what is the 'it' that is raining. Such phenomena as lightning, wind, rain, and so on, are transitional cases between what would be clearly labelled with a noun by all men (e.g., dog, tree, etc.) and what would not. It is not, therefore, surprising that different cultures refer to these phenomena differently. (For further discussion see Bolinger, ch. 13; Landar, ch. 5.)

If language is an important factor in helping us to shape experience then, since it is the shaping of experience that gives meaning to the stimuli that impinge upon us from the environment, the language that we use helps to determine what meaning life will have for us. All human communities possess language, and the most primitive communities in existence today possess languages that are linguistically more complex than those of the civilised nations. This fact makes it very difficult to account for the origin of language from onomatopeic speech sounds (the 'bow-wow theory'), instinctive emotional cries (the 'pooh-pooh theory'), instinctive relationships between internal impressions and the speech sounds to which they give rise (the 'ding-dong theory'), and innate sounds made in the course of muscular effort (the 'yo-heave-ho theory' or 'yo-he-ho' as it is usually given). The apparent hopelessness of ever arriving at a solution of the origin of language caused the Société de Linguistique of Paris to ban papers on this topic early in the present century. Whatever the eventual solution of the problem we must accept the fact that coherent language is part of man's biological inheritance. (For further discussion see Barber, Hockett, and Pei, 1952 and 1962.)

Whatever the origin of language we may accept De Saussure's view that language, as we find it existing, consists of symbols that are arbitrary (in that there is no necessary connection between a word and what it symbolises) and constant (in that all members of a group use the word in the same way). The difficulty of recognising the arbitrary nature of linguistic symbols is experienced by most people learning their first foreign languages, who find it difficult to understand why the French refer to bread as *pain* and the Germans as *Brot*. The Greeks considered that all who did not speak Greek were simply mouthing sounds like 'bar-bar' (hence they called them 'barbarians'); and the Germans' word for their own language (*Deutsch*) may be connected with the verb 'to mean' (*bedeuten*), which suggests that the early Germans thought of their language as the only one that was meaningful (Bett). In order to understand the relationships of language to meaning one must step outside language as it were, which is why the study of language from this point of view is called *meta*linguistics.

In common with other scientists, the linguists who study language and culture eschew value judgements. This attitude has led to the rather uncomfortable situation in which the word 'culture' in the vocabulary of these scientists refers to the social structure of the simplest communities, whereas for most other people it applies to the sophisticated products of advanced societies. One reason for this may be the preference of these linguists for spoken, rather than written forms, for which they have been criticised by Pei (1962). Whatever the reason for their restricted use of the term, the fact remains that, when linguists talk of 'culture', they do not mean what others mean by the term. The same is true of the sociologists who like to describe the current manifestations of musical puerility as 'pop culture', making it necessary to coin the term 'high culture' for references to art and literature.

For a discussion of the relationships between language and life-style in societies more advanced than those of the American Indians one must usually seek elsewhere. One writer who has contributed to this topic is Goad, who discusses the correspondence between language and mental habits in the context of history and national character. From this point of view Goad treats some of the major international languages and their role in historical progress, from classical Greek and Latin to modern English. With specific regard to 'high culture' there is a current view, associated with the writings of George Steiner, that language has become corrupted, and is no longer as suitable for dealing with reality as other forms of symbolism, e.g., mathematics. (For a critique of Steiner's view see Newton-de Molina, 1969.)

The philosophers who have attempted to demonstrate the influence of language structure upon philosophical misunderstandings are represented in Britain by Ayer and Ryle, who have been extremely influential. In *Language, Truth and Logic* Ayer placed great emphasis on the fact that Indo-European sentences are constructed in terms of subject and predicate, so that what is in the predicate is regarded as the attribute of the subject. This leads us to suppose that in every sentence constructed in this way the subject *must* have the attributes mentioned in the predicate. Thus in saying 'I exist', *existence* is predicated of *I*. However, it would be wrong to suppose that existence is an attribute; this error had led people to argue, for example, that because God is perfect and must therefore have all attributes, He must have the attribute of existence, i.e., He must exist. It is now generally accepted (since the work of G. E. Moore) that existence is not an attribute. Ayer considers that all metaphysical disputes similarly arose from a misuse of language, a view shared by the Oxford group of philosophers to which Ayer belongs. (We shall consider Ayer's views on the question of meaning in Chapter 11.)

In *The Concept of Mind* Ryle applied this style of argument to psychological concepts. Whilst it would be inappropriate to discuss all Ryle's arguments here, it is important to illustrate his main theme. What Ryle is trying to do is to display some of the errors that arise from a misuse of words. The sort of misuse that he has in mind is not a grammatical misuse but a logical misuse. The main set of errors that he wishes to discuss are those relating to our talk of body and mind. These errors he said arise from a Cartesian myth. It is possibly a little unfair to blame Descartes for many of the errors that have arisen as a result of the misuse of the terms body and mind, and Ryle does admit that Descartes was merely codifying ideas that were prevalent at the time. However he goes on to say that Descartes was doing this partly in order to bring the understanding of the mind into line with the Galilean understanding of the physical universe. For our purposes the reason for Descartes's usage of terms 'body' and 'mind' is not particularly important. If we think of the universe as composed of bodies and minds and we want to know what is the difference between them, we can say that bodies are extended in space and they exist over periods of time. Minds in somewhat the same way exist over periods of time but they are not extended in space. The idea thus arose that body is extended stuff and mind is not extended stuff, existing only in time. If we now go on to ask questions about the relations between body and mind we find we are getting into a number of difficulties. One might ask, for example, 'How is it that my will, which belongs to my mind, can determine that I shall lift my arm? What is the connection between them?' We have to assume that there is some interaction between body and mind and Descartes even designated the pineal gland as the site of this interaction. The questions that we ask about interactions between bodies and minds are virtually unanswerable. This is fairly serious in itself, but there is an even more serious consequence of this use of terms and it is this, that if I assume that the mind is not extended in space and is therefore not observable by anyone apart from the person who actually has that mind then I cannot know any mind other than my own; indeed there are no grounds for my believing that there is any mind other than my own, and there is no one to confirm my experiences: everything therefore may be a figment of my imagination. This view is known as *solipsism*. Whilst one may draw perfectly logical conclusions from Cartesian principles to establish the validity of solipsism, it is not reasonable for one to assume that there is no one in the universe but oneself. Now since this is so, it means that there is something funny about the philosophy, because this philosophy is leading to conclusions that are not demonstrable, but seem to be nonsensical in view of the vast accumulation of every-day experience. How, then, has this error arisen? What is more important, how are we going to rephrase our terms so that this error no longer arises? This is the problem that Gilbert Ryle has set himself in *The Concept of Mind*.

Ryle argues that to talk of minds in the same way as to talk of bodies is to commit a logical category error, that is to say, we talk about things as if they belonged in one category when in fact they belong to another category. Sometimes we may deliberately misuse words for humorous effect for example: 'She changed her mind and the sheets'. This would be an obvious example of a category error, because minds and sheets are not in the same category. It is not immediately clear that minds and bodies are not in the same category, but Ryle argues that it is indeed the case. He says, Imagine we were showing someone around the university, we would show this visitor all the buildings, we would show him some students, some lecturers, and possibly even the Vice-Chancellor, and then the person would say 'All right, I have seen the buildings, the students, the staff and the Vice-Chancellor, now show me the university'. Now this is like watching all the soldiers in a regiment march past and saying 'Well I've seen all the soldiers now where's the regiment?' If a person spoke in this way and asked these sorts of questions, we should have to conclude that he did not know how to use the words 'university' and 'regiment' respectively. Ryle argues that philosophers have been guilty of misusing the word 'mind' in somewhat the same way as this unlettered person of our example was misusing the words 'university' and 'regiment'. Ryle argues that when we say of someone that his mind caused him to behave in this way we are talking as if there were a little ghost inside a machine, directing the machine how to behave. Now we do not assume that there are ghosts inside machines causing them to behave, but Ryle argues that to talk of minds and bodies as we have done traditionally, is to assume that there is something rather like a ghost inside the body telling the body how to behave. Of course, if we do take this point of view, someone can quite legitimately ask 'Well, how do you know there is not a little ghost inside the ghost telling the ghost how to behave?' One can go back *ad infinitum* looking for little ghosts telling other little ghosts how to behave. Clearly this is not a very satisfactory state of affairs and so Ryle argues that we should stop using our words as if we were referring to ghosts in machines.

At the present time the style of philosophy expounded by Ayer and Ryle seems a little naive (for a critique see Gellner). However, this is not a text in philosophy, but one in psychology, so we must limit ourselves to the observation that the use of language is a concern that draws together linguists, psychologists, philosophers and others.

Among the others we must include sociologists, represented in this respect by Bernstein (1961a, 1961b), who has drawn attention to the differing linguistic conventions of different social classes. Bernstein maintains that the relationship between social structure and individual experience is a major theoretical problem of common concern to psychologists and sociologists, because language is conditioned by social structure, yet it mediates individual experience.

Bernstein points out that different social groups (whether of occupation, status, or any other criterion) use different forms of linguistic expression. An individual growing up in a group will learn the linguistic forms favoured by that group; these forms will then be used to elicit and strengthen the ways of thinking and feeling pertaining to that group.

If we consider the linguistic behaviour of an individual we find that he may select his modes of expression from a wide range of utterances, so that his linguistic behaviour will be relatively unpredictable: or he may select from a narrow range, thus making his utterances relatively predictable. In the former case he is said to use an *elaborated code*: in the second we say that he uses a *restricted code*. Whether an individual adopts an elaborated or a restricted code will depend upon an individual's social background and on his purposes in speaking; obviously a poor educational background will make it difficult for an individual to use an elaborated code, but even a well-educated person will frequently use a restricted code.

The term 'restricted' is misleading if it suggests that a restricted code cannot be used for purposes of communication. A restricted code may be *pure* (as in cocktail-party gambits) or *public*. The public form of a restricted code is used for everyday communication between members of social groups, different groups using different public restricted codes. This means that members of a social group will understand each other, but will have difficulty in understanding members of other social groups. Different social groups may even perceive events differently, because language picks out relevant features of experience. The public form of a language that a child learns in a social group serves to direct his attention away from stimuli that are not significant, and towards those stimuli that are.

The poorer socio-economic groups tend to be limited to a severely restricted linguistic code, which is impersonal in the sense that it cannot easily express emotions; this means that emotions must be expressed by the intonation of the voice. Moreover a restricted code cannot easily express fine shades of difference of perception and opinion, which makes it difficult for the individual limited to such a code to solve problems involving a high degree of abstraction, for which an elaborated code is required.

Bernstein draws many more conclusions about the differences between social groups based upon their differing linguistic usages, including their methods of socialisation, their emotional responses, and their relative tendencies to authoritarian or democratic structure. These are not our immediate concern. Enough has been said, however, to indicate that misunderstandings between social groups may arise from language, which can thus serve to hamper, rather than facilitate, communication.

In view of all the confusions to which the use of language can give rise, it is a matter of some astonishment that human beings understand each other as well as they do. Despite Voltaire's remark that 'language was given to man to disguise his thoughts' the fact remains that we *do* communicate with each other.

We communicate with each other not only by language but also by images. When we dream we communicate with ourselves by images. It is to the study of imagery that we turn in the next chapter.

5

MENTAL IMAGERY

The term 'imagery' has a variety of meanings. It may refer to iconic representations such as paintings and sculpture, or to the form of words used by a poet to suggest a mood. Rituals are said to employ imagery to the extent that they incorporate symbolic representations of spiritual matters; and, inasmuch as myths are the representation, in narrative form, of spiritual truths, they also incorporate imagery. All these topics are both interesting and important, but they are not primarily the concern of psychologists. The main interest of psychologists in this regard is in the images of the world held by individuals rather than social groups. We may, for want of a better term, call this *mental* imagery.

Like so much else that contemporary psychology has neglected to its loss, the study of mental imagery was begun by Sir Francis Galton, who thought that a study of this imagery might illustrate essential differences between the 'mental operations of different men', as he put it, and afford a clue to the origin of mystical visions. To this end he sent out a questionnaire to large numbers of people, asking his respondents to elaborate their replies in letters. The questions to which he sought answers concerned the illumination, definition and colouring of his subjects' mental images, for example of their breakfast table.

Of the subjects questioned, most of the scientists denied having imagery. 'They had no more notion of its true nature than a colour-blind man, who has not discerned his defect, has of the nature of colour.' Among the general public the results were quite different. Many men, and more women, also boys and girls, professed to having distinct, coloured mental imagery.

By sending his questionnaires abroad Galton obtained results from all over the world. As some people (not only abroad, but also at home) did not reply, his sample was probably not random, but among those who did reply there was a high measure of agreement between patterns of replies from schools and from individual correspondents. From the responses Galton was able to draw two conclusions. First, that it was possible to obtain psychological insights into the minds of others: secondly, 'scientific men, as a class, have feeble powers of visual representation'.

Because scientists had less vivid visual imagery than non-scientists Galton supposed that vivid imagery was antagonistic to the development of abstract thinking. Nevertheless, he argued, the highest minds have probably not lost the faculty of visual imagery, but have subordinated it to other modes of thinking, retaining it for use on suitable occasions. He also recognised that some people characteristically employ auditory, rather than visual imagery, whilst others employ kinaesthetic imagery, i.e., sensations in the muscles corresponding to the action of those muscles in carrying out the relevant actions.

Inasmuch as our main concern here is with the relation of imagery to thinking, rather than with imagery as such, we shall not summarise all of Galton's findings. From our point of view the most important observation is that Galton found no special relationship between 'high visualising power and the intellectual faculties', although he realised that it would be a great help in certain professions (particularly that of mechanical inventor). One curious fact is that Napoleon believed that strong visualisers made poor generals, although his reasons for this belief are not known.

Galton considered that 'our bookish and wordy education tends to repress this valuable gift of nature', and that we should seriously study 'the best way of developing and utilising this faculty, without prejudice to the practice of abstract thought in symbols'.

Imagery is not, of course, synonymous with imagination. Imagery is usually spontaneous and comes without effort, whereas imagination, whether creative or pathological, requires some cognitive effort on the part of the imaginer. Clearly, however, imagery is one source from which the individual can draw for his imagination. The relationships between imagery and thinking are therefore of considerable interest to psychologists, and have been discussed at some length by McKellar, who distinguishes six major types of imagery.

1. *Ordinary waking images* (the sort studied by Galton).
2. *Dream images*, which are typically visual, although auditory and kinaesthetic dreams occasionally occur.
3. *Eidetic imagery*, which is the ability to project one's visual images

on to a surface and view them like a photograph. This was first studied by Jaensch. It bears no relation to intelligence, but is found more often in children than in adults. Some adults have this faculty whilst being of very low intelligence, the so-called *idiots savants*; on the other hand some highly intelligent scientists have been strong imagers. One psychologist who was gifted in this way was Titchener, who boasted of having strong auditory and kinaesthetic imagery which, combined with eidetic imagery, helped him in the delivery of his lectures.

4. *Waking-sleeping imagery*, which is of two kinds. The *hypnagogic* state occurs just before one falls asleep; the *hypnopompic* state is the half-asleep state that occurs just before one awakes fully. Visual and auditory modes are common. One notable feature particularly of the hypnagogic state is the concretisation of thought; for instance, a mathematician thinking before going to sleep of a problem involving a^2 may have a strong image of a market square. (The most celebrated case is that of Kekulé, who solved the problem of the benzene ring structure when dozing after lunch before the fire: he suddenly had an image of a snake swallowing its own tail.) The hypnopompic state is a prolongation of the dream state into the period of wakefulness, so that one is apt to confuse images with reality.

5. *Crystal images*. Many people 'see' images in surfaces like crystal balls; these images can often be induced by suggestion or drugs.

6. *Hallucinations*. There is no sharp distinction between images and hallucinations. The distinction is one of degree, and is related to other known facts about the individual: for instance, schizophrenics characteristically hear voices commanding them to do things, whereas alcoholics have visual hallucinations. Probably everyone has hallucinations from time to time, and their occurrence is not, by itself, indicative of abnormality.

Of these forms of imagery, the types that occur in sleep, and between sleeping and full consciousness, are of particular interest to the psychologist, because they seem to reveal a primitive type of thinking, which is opposed to the abstract thinking characteristic of conscious cognitive effort. McKellar calls it 'autistic' thinking as opposed to 'reality-adjusted' thinking. Although we all display some autistic thinking whilst we are awake (for instance, when daydreaming) for the most part our thinking is under realistic control. When we fall asleep the control weakens, and we exhibit the more primitive characteristics of fantasy, concretisation, and so on. In many ways the schizophrenic is like someone who, whilst awake, displays the thinking characteristic of someone who is asleep, a fact remarked upon by Jung. A study of dreams is therefore of considerable interest for the light it can shed on pathological thinking.[1]

Dreams can also illuminate problems of the normal personality, as Freud established. Freud regarded dreams as deriving from normal mental functioning in such a way that their *manifest* content disguised a *latent* content, which was the product of unconscious psychic forces. Later workers who have attempted to disprove Freud's contention that unresolved conflicts help to shape dreams have usually overlooked Freud's distinction between manifest and latent content: in many cases they have discovered in dreams the residue of the day's sensory experience, and have argued that this residue rather than unresolved conflicts provides the material for dreams. Freud would certainly have agreed that this residue provided material for the manifest content (in fact he stated that the source of the dream material was *always* the previous day's experiences); but investigations of this kind are irrelevant to the question of latent content.

A different sort of criticism of Freud is made by Fromm, who objects to Freud's emphasis on the irrational 'lower' nature of man, arguing instead that dreams may express the highest as well as the lowest human aspirations. Both Freud and Fromm agree that dreams can shed light on unconscious motivation, and are an important means of understanding the personality. Both, too, agree that the study of myths sheds light on human nature, although they disagree over the interpretation of the myths, Freud favouring an interpretation in terms of sexual, and particularly incestuous, strivings, Fromm seeing in such myths as that of Oedipus the struggle between matriarchal and patriarchal organisations of society.

We have said that the schizophrenic exhibits in his waking life the sort of thinking that normal people exhibit when they dream. Unfortunately it is difficult to discover very much about dreaming, because we forget the great majority of our dreams, remembering for the most part only fragments of the last dreams that we have before awakening. Therefore some psychologists have found it convenient to employ drugs to induce in volunteers temporary symptoms of psychosis. These drugs include mescaline, lysergic acid diethylamide (LSD-25) and nitrous oxide. There is one major difference between the temporary disorders induced by these methods and schizophrenia, namely that drug-induced hallucinations are predominantly visual, whereas those of schizophrenia are characteristically auditory. Nevertheless the nature of the thought disorder

[1] For a review of mental ability during sleep see Foulkes.

induced by drugs is important in suggesting the possible nature of thought disorder in schizophrenia.

Subjects taking these drugs under experimental conditions report that the mind frequently 'goes blank', and that there may be a profound suspicion of the questioners. The similarity of this state to that of psychotics is illustrated by the work of Clifford Beers, who wrote an autobiography describing his own lengthy breakdown and his recovery from it, and helped to establish the mental hygiene movement in America.

Beers had attempted to commit suicide, but he imagined himself to be charged with various crimes, arson being among them. He believed that the asylum was a police institution (or, as Beers put it, 'part of the Third Degree') in which not only the doctors and attendants, but also the other patients, were detectives. Some of them resembled the principals or victims of the crimes with which he imagined himself to be charged. All the remarks overheard in conversation appeared to refer to these crimes and to his own part in them. Moreover, although he longed to read, he would not do so because all printed matter seemed to refer to the crimes, and to read about them without protesting his innocence would be to incriminate himself and other people. This condition illustrates what are called 'delusions of self-reference'.

Another feature is that of too many ideas flooding into consciousness to permit following a train of thought. This has been likened to the inability to follow a melody when one is simultaneously fully aware of all the parts in the harmony. Normally the mind selects and organises incoming information, suppressing some aspects in order to make overall sense of the whole, in other words it pays attention selectively. If the power of paying attention is lost, the result is confusion. Every word that we use has a multitude of associations, and the power of selective attention is normally exercised in order to select only those associations that permit an orderly sequence of thinking. If the schizophrenic has indeed lost the power of suppressing unwanted associations, then one can well understand the utter confusion of his thoughts.

This confusion would help to account for two further features of schizophrenic thinking. These are the so-called 'knight's move' thinking, in which, instead of following a conventional logical sequence, the schizophrenic's thinking appears to exhibit discontinuities because it follows a devious path through unlikely associations: and 'paralogical thinking', in which the sequence of thoughts makes sense, but not conventional sense. This may be illustrated by the case of an intelligent schizophrenic known to the author, who announced one day that she must become an air hostess, after seeing an advertisement for Pan-American Airways, because her elder brother was called Peter and her younger sister Wendy. The association of ideas 'Peter Pan and Wendy' suggested that, as the middle one of the family, she must be the Pan referred to on the poster.

A second account from Beers will further illustrate bizarre associations. In Beers' room the gas jet was situated at some distance from his bed, so when it was necessary for the physician to lock the muff that Beers had to wear to prevent further suicide attempts an attendant had to stand by with a lighted candle. One night the physician said: 'You won't try again to do what you did in New Haven, will you?' The physician was referring to Beers' attempted suicide by jumping from an upper-storey window, but Beers did not realise this until many months later. At the time when the muff was being locked Beers was struck by a similarity between the doctor's name and that of a man whose trial for arson Beers had once attended out of curiosity, and at the same time observed the candle held by the attendant. These circumstances led Beers to imagine that he was in some way connected with that crime, and that he was an accomplice. It was to this, rather than the suicide attempt, to which he believed the doctor to be referring.

Finally we may draw a parallel between the schizophrenic and the creative artist. The artist is aware of more associations to words and objects than the average person, but he is able to select unlikely associations for his own purposes. Unlike the schizophrenic the artist is able to impose realistic controls on his autistic thought processes (see Ghiselin). As to what causes people to differ in their power to control associations many theories have been proposed concerning brain physiology, the most important of which is that serotonin, a substance similar in its effects to LSD-25 and mescaline, occurs naturally in the nervous system of schizophrenics. However, as with all proposed physiological explanations of psychosis, the evidence is not strong. Even if it were the case that serotonin in the brain was associated with schizophrenic thinking, this would only explain an imbalance in reality-adjusted and autistic thinking and would not account for the existence side by side of two thought processes; nor would it explain their balance in normal individuals.

(The topic of creativity is further discussed in Chapter 8. For a recent survey of the topic of mental imagery see Richardson.)

Let us conclude by speculating on the possible significance of the existence of two thought processes, one being the familiar rationality of waking life, the other a parallel process, with a logic of its own, which takes over when we daydream or when we sleep. This second process is always present, ready to break through the barriers of our rationality in the form of fears, superstitions, and bizarre behaviour. The Freudian explanation of these regrettable phenomena is in terms of repression into the unconscious of primitive drives, particularly those of sex and aggression, a view rejected by Fromm, as we have seen. In historical retrospect it does seem that Freud was a little too inclined to emphasise man's lower nature: unfortunately Fromm, with his emphasis on the matriarchy/patriarchy struggle, is equally one-sided.

Some insight into the problem may be yielded by considering the possible origins of symbolism. Piaget gives the example of a young child, attempting to force an object into a box with a narrow opening, who opened her mouth wide to mimic the opening of the box. Piaget (1951, etc.) sees such actions, which represent interactions with the environment, as the origin of symbolism, when the actions become internalised and implicit. (This view of imagery as the internalisation of action parallels Luria's view of thinking as the internalisation of spoken language: see Chapter 9.) Whilst this may not be the entire truth, it is probably the case that much symbolism originated in man's attempts to come to terms with the world around him. Even today the most learned physicists frequently find it necessary to construct models to facilitate comprehension of their own abstruse theories, so it should not surprise us if primitive man found it necessary to construct representations of his world in an attempt to come to terms with it, and that, with the development of more sophisticated tools such as language and mathematics, such early attempts at mastery became overlaid in human consciousness.

The experience of primitive man must surely have been that poetically expressed by the lines 'I, a stranger and afraid, In a world I never made'. The rituals, and later the religions, of early man, were no doubt motivated by this fear. Only at a late stage in human evolution did a rational approach to the universe appear, and it was a tenuous growth, easily choked by the weeds of superstition that followed the fall of Greece. Twentieth-century man has inherited such a legacy of fear, superstition, and intellectual blackness that it is probably an oversimplification to explain the existence of irrationality entirely in terms of the repression of sexual and aggressive drives, important though these undoubtedly are. (For a history of irrational notions see Castiglioni.)

Imagery, then, has two origins: superstitious fear of a strange world, and primitive attempts to make sense of that world. Modern man cannot be fully rational all the time, and in his irrational moments imagery from both sources is likely to break through into awareness. The fact that this imagery can, in the case of creative thinkers, be used in the service of the intellect should not lead us to suppose that the study of imagery will necessarily lead us to higher truth. Such study may, indeed, lead us to wisdom, not, as Fromm and others suppose, because it illuminates the truth, but because it shows us the dark places to avoid.

6

SYMBOLISM AND PLAY

We shall discuss in Chapter 9 the process whereby we organise our experienced world into conceptual schemes. Often to make life easier for ourselves we summarise a conceptual scheme by a word, which is then responded to as having meaning in its own right rather than as symbolic of a deeper reality. Benjamin Lee Whorf pointed out that people will often overlook the dangerous aspects of a situation because the situation is described in terms that do not carry a connotation of danger: for instance workers will be very careful about smoking when they see a notice reading 'petrol drums' but less careful if the notice reads 'empty petrol drums', although the residues of petrol vapour make the situation hazardous, because the word 'empty' is synonymous with 'null and void' and hence suggests no danger. The notice 'empty petrol drums' signifies an absence of petrol but is responded to as if it meant an absence of everything.

As we said in Chapter 4 Whorf believed that habitual language shapes our perception of the world in which we live and hence our behaviour in that world. Stated in this way the notion seems too crude to be true. However, if we interpet it to mean that a word can help to determine which conceptual scheme among many will control our conduct, then Whorf's point is well taken. The reaction to the notice 'empty petrol drums' would not be the same if one understood that 'empty' *in this context* did not signify absence of petrol vapour, as it would if one did not understand this. In other words our behaviour is shaped not by the symbol but by what it symbolises. Behaviour *directly* controlled by words or other symbols would be truly pathological.

Similar confusion between symbols and conceptual schemes is exhibited by Wagner, when he quotes the case of a woman hospitalised for an allergy to milk who was found, in the words of the physician, to be sensitive 'to the word "milk" ' (*On the Wisdom of Words*, pp. 148–9). The woman would exhibit allergic sensitivity to water if she was told that it was milk. It would probably be more accurate to say that the patient was sensitive to the *concept* of milk, and that the word 'milk' activated this concept and the behaviour associated with it. (Cases such as this may help to explain the familiar placebo reaction, whereby about one-third of patients will respond to an inert substance if they believe that it is a drug.)

Language is not the only symbolic form to activate conceptual schemes; pictorial representation, sometimes combined with words, can also do this. An example was provided by an article in the London *Sunday Times* for 27 September 1970, which reported that complaints had been made that a poster showing a pannier-full of 'Fresh Farm Eggs' was being used to advertise battery-farm eggs. In defence the publicity manager of the Egg Marketing Board was quoted as saying: 'It is simply a pictorial piece of display without the intention of applying specifically or solely to any one method of husbandry. *And hens in a field look nicer than in battery formation.*'[1]

This is a case of symbolic representation becoming more important than the reality it symbolises. Unfortunately such errors are more frequent than one would wish, although they are not all as sinister as the one quoted, with its implication that truth is irrelevant so long as one creates a good impression. Wagner quotes an amusing example of the Irish determination to use the Irish tongue whenever possible, and to encourage its use in commerce. Some years ago plastic leprechauns were sold in Dublin bearing a notice in Irish which, when translated read 'Made in Japan'.

The fact that we organise our conscious experience into conceptual schemes helps to explain many puzzling and apparently irrational elements of our behaviour, for example, prejudice. We react to other people according to whether they belong to our categories of 'acceptable' or 'unacceptable'. The categories themselves may have been transmitted to us by other people through the medium of language, or they may have been built up as the result of experiences of different people who may have had in common one incidental characteristic, which has come to symbolise for us the characteristics of the whole group. This symbol may or may not be verbalised. If it is verbalised, the verbalisation may be incorrect in the sense that the wrong feature has been labelled. Thus one may say that he does not like a particular group of people because they are dirty, when deeper analysis will reveal that his dislike arises from

[1] Author's italics.

his feelings of inferiority in face of this group. It is well known that highly prejudiced individuals may express mutually contradictory opinions about the objects of their dislike. (See Adorno *et al.* for the investigation of prejudice.) An extreme example of words taking the place of reason to such an extent as to blind their users occurred in Nazi Germany, when the favoured race was Nordic, with fair hair and blue eyes. The Nazi leaders did not look like this, but that did not prevent them from regarding themselves as Nordic 'types'.

A less extreme example is found in the ways in which a complex situation can be designated as belonging to a particular category and subsequent behaviour be determined by the general features of the chosen category rather than by the true facts of the situation. Thus when airliners were recently seized by force of arms and their passengers held as hostages for the release of captured guerillas, a number of statesmen appeared on television urging the government not to give in to 'blackmail'. The word in this context seems ill-chosen, for the blackmailer's strength lies in the fact that he knows that his victim has something to hide and fears disclosure, whereas in the case under discussion the government had nothing to hide and there was no question of disclosing anything. This is not a pedantic quibble because it raises a serious issue, namely that the arguments put forward by many leading figures about 'not giving in' were very cogent in a case presented as one of blackmail, but less evidently relevant to a case of kidnapping and demanding ransom. Thus the choice of an inappropriate word to describe the situation caused the speakers to adduce arguments in favour of inappropriate action. Examples of this sort could be multiplied. In the degree of confusion that they exhibit they fall somewhere between Whorf's example of the empty petrol drums and the racial myths of 'Nordic types'.[1]

Common to all the examples quoted is a lack of flexibility of thinking brought about by the activated conceptual scheme. Sometimes this can have grisly consequences. For instance a certain religious group at one time used to execute offenders by decapitating them in a kneeling position, with the result that the headless bodies slumped to the ground. It was decided that this was inconsistent with the dignity of the body and hence inhumane, so the method of execution was changed to that of pouring boiling lead down the victim's throats. The fact that this greatly increased the suffering of the criminals was seemingly less important than the consideration that the execution was more dignified. Koestler (1967) quotes many examples which

[1] One may also be misled by words about words. In Kinsey's obituary it was said that '. . . sex, for him, was not a four-letter word'.

suggest that man is inherently insane, but he appears to have over-looked this one.

Alberto C. Blanc reports on the practice of eating the brains of one's enemies, which has been practised by man since the earliest times, and which was possibly a legacy from hominid ancestors. In recent times governmental action to stamp out this practice amongst the headhunters of Borneo was opposed by the natives because the warriors would kill an enemy, then cook his brains at a ceremonial feast at which they would pass on the enemy warrior's name to one of their own children. Their objection to attempts to stop the practice was that, if they did not eat their enemies' brains, they would no longer be able to name their children.[1]

A lack of flexibility in one or more respects of life is exhibited by all individuals and societies, and Moreno saw a loss of spontaneity as the inevitable result of cultural progress. Societies, being large, cumbersome institutions are inherently less flexible than individuals, and if an individual conducted his life on the principles adopted by national states in their international relations, he would soon be hospitalised on the ground of criminal insanity. However, there is a type of individual whom it is instructive to consider here, who though not necessarily criminal, and certainly not insane, is never-theless dangerous. This is the schizoid individual. The term is ill-chosen, as it suggests a form of schizophrenia, which it is not. The schizoid individual is one in whom direct feelings for others are absent. He runs his life according to intellectual schemes from which human considerations may be entirely absent. Such individuals usually have enormous energy, and frequently manage to obtain positions of great administrative power, which they exercise with a ruthlessness that betrays their lack of humanity. It is likely that the schizoid mentality is a transient feature of normal adolescence, and that the schizoid adult is one who has not matured in this respect. This might account for the ease with which some dictators recruit followers from the young.

The fact that we organise much of our life according to conceptual schemes does not of itself indicate pathology. Symbols of patriotism give rise to national pride, which helps a country to survive in times of war and danger. Once the danger has passed the symbols remain to give emotional satisfaction to those who have lived through the danger, whilst appearing ridiculous to the generation that has not. Conversely the symbols of those adolescents who have nothing to contribute to culture but their youth appear ludicrous to the mature.

[1] For a discussion of the related problem of the symbolic significance of the skull see Henschen.

Such conflict probably testifies to nothing more serious than that the society in which the conflicts take place is not moribund.

The importance of symbolic activity is most clearly revealed when it is lost. In Chapter 11 we shall discuss the effect of brain damage on the ability to employ discursive symbols, whilst in Chapter 5 we saw that schizophrenics had difficulty in interpreting the symbolic significance of objects and events. Less drastic and more common than either is the neurotic symptom of feeling that everything is 'meaningless'. Such a reaction could not occur if the patient did not normally regard things, persons, and events as having a significance of which they are symbolic. Loss of this power to see things as symbolic of a deeper reality leads the sufferer to perceive surface relationships only. This symbolic view of the universe is so natural to us that we are seldom aware of it until it is lost.

The intimate connection between symbols and reality is attested to by the common experience that we do not truly know the common flowers and trees in our garden until we have learnt their names. Children, of course, want to know the name of everything. This urge to attach names to things suggests that, for man, reality *is* symbols.

Symbolic ability can be disturbed in two ways. Either one can mistake the symbol for reality (as in our example of the Egg Marketing Board) or one can argue, with McLuhan and his kith, that appearance is all. With regard to the second it may be significant that the recent series of Promenade Concerts featured a group called 'The Soft Machine',[1] one of whose members wore a shift bearing the legend 'Stamp out Reality'. For an appearance in a cultural event this was no doubt an appropriate slogan.

The loss of symbolic ability has been singled out as the major pathology of our society, leading to feelings of alienation. Thus Laing in a number of books, of which the most coherent is probably *The Politics of Experience,* argues that we have lost touch with our inner experience, and that consequently our interpersonal behaviour is disruptive. Critics of McLuhan have accused him of being characteristically antihuman in denying any distinction between medium and message, and seeing only surface relationships (see Chapter 4). The contemporary French fiction of Robbe-Grillet and others encounters the same accusation (see Wagner for a discussion of this fiction).

If we attempt to relate these diverse tendencies to the issues to be discussed later in Chapter 14 we may oversimplify the situation by regarding the overvaluation of surface relationships as in the sceptical tradition of the empiricists, whilst the belief that appear-

[1] Possibly a type of Glockenspiel.

ances and media are symbolic of underlying realities is in the tradition of rationalism. Behaviourism, being in the empiricist tradition, is bitterly attacked by rationalists such as Chomsky and Koch, the length and vitriolic nature of their arguments being frequently more impressive than their cogency. This bitterness is commented upon unfavourably by Broadbent, who points out that the arguments of the empiricists are usually much calmer than those of their critics. As he says: 'I would just say that I think the advantage in human sensitivity and ethics lies with the empiricists and not with their opponents.'

There are two points that one may make in answer to this. In the first place the equanimity of the behaviourists may possibly be accounted for by the lines: 'if you can keep your head whilst those about you are losing theirs, you probably don't know what's going on'. What is going on according to some critics is that civilisation and culture as we know them are rapidly being eroded, and it is tempting to see the seeds of this erosion in the empiricist psychology that denies the value of imagery, symbols, and so on. The second point is that being a behaviourist does not make one proof against making extreme allegations about one's opponents. Thus Mowrer (1961) argues that morality is being undermined, and virtually accuses Freud of having made a pact with Satan, whereby Freud would attack the power of conscience in return for being enabled to overcome his attacks of depression. Mowrer writes as follows: 'Today no one, of course, "believes" in the Devil in the sense in which he was conceived in the Middle Ages. Instead we have come to "believe" in Freud and psychoanalysis. But now we are confronted by the astonishing possibility that Freud and his works are the twentieth-century equivalent of the Devil, thinly disguised.'

On reading Freud and his works one is impressed by how aptly chosen the adjective 'astonishing' is. It is probably true that those who wish to attack morality can quote from Freud for support, but the fact that the Devil can quote scripture for his own purposes does not mean that the Devil wrote the scriptures. Freud was a highly moral man, and to use his work to attack morality is a perversion of psychoanalysis.

It is certainly true that moral standards have changed since Freud's day, and it will be helpful to look at these changes, which have been reviewed, as far as the USA is concerned, by Wolfenstein. From an examination of *Infant Care* (the Bulletin of the Children's Bureau) for the periods 1914–21, 1929–38, and 1942–5 she detects a change from the earlier view that children had strong autoerotic urges requiring stern suppression, to the view that play is not just permissible but necessary for healthy development. The earlier distinction between the child's desires and his needs has been replaced by the view that 'what is pleasant is also good for you' (Marie Lloyd would doubtless have agreed). The consequence of the new view is that 'what the baby wants for pleasure has thus become as legitimate a demand as what he needs for his physical well-being and is to be treated in the same way'. Similarly appetite is now relied upon as a guide to feeling.

The change in the attitudes to the child's impulses, from regarding them as dangerous to indulging them, are related to play, because 'where impulses are dangerous and the good and pleasant are opposed, play is suspect'. In 1914 playing with the baby was condemned as tending to harm the child's health, but 'play is now to be fused with all the activities of life'. The mother is urged to make all her child-rearing activities fun for herself and her baby. 'Play, having ceased to be wicked, having become harmless and good, now becomes a new duty.' Now that fun has become not only permissible but required, mothers who do not feel that every aspect of child-rearing is fun frequently feel guilty. The stress on fun thus has its own obligations, which differ from those of the old morality.

These changing attitudes are related to widely diffused values in western culture. 'From having dreaded impulses and being worried about whether conscience was adequate to cope with them, we have come round to finding conscience a nuisance and worrying about the adequacy of our impulses.' The ability to have fun is becoming an important factor in personnel selection,[1] so play has become work.

The picture painted by Wolfenstein at first sight appears to give support to Mowrer's fear that devils are abroad in western culture, but Wolfenstein suggests that the emphasis on play is a new form of defence against impulses, which works by diluting them.

On reading the minor Victorian comic novelists (e.g., Jerome and the Grossmiths) one frequently has the impression that men and women of that age enjoyed play more than we do today, as if the separation of play from work made both more intense. That this is not just an illusion is confirmed by the studies of Huizinga, who feels that the element of pure play is declining or becoming distorted in contemporary culture. With the increasing amount of professionalism – overt and covert – in sport, play is indeed becoming work. In the arts, says Huizinga, 'a convulsive craving for originality distorts the creative impulse': the play element in art is now to be found in 'the modern apparatus of publicity, with its puffy art-

[1] At least in the USA. The pressure for the adoption of this criterion is, however, probably growing in Britain.

criticism, exhibitions and lectures'. In politics the element of sophisticated play has been declining since the eighteenth century. Unfortunately the loss here has not been compensated by an increasing professionalism, but has been replaced by 'puerilism . . . a blend of adolescence and barbarity which has been rampant all over the world for the last two or three decades . . . . It would seem as if the mentality and conduct of the adolescent now reigned supreme.'

Caillois has extended Huizinga's views on the corruption of games, and has made an analysis of games the basis of a sociology. Caillois divides games into four types, based respectively on competition, chance, mimicry, and the pursuit of vertigo. Each may exist in cultural, institutional, or corrupt forms. Thus a cultural form of competition is the familiar sporting event; its institutional form is economic competition and competitive examination; the corrupt form is violence, trickery and the will to power. Games of chance exist in cultural form as lotteries; in institutional form as stock-market speculation; in corrupt form as superstition, astrology, etc. The cultural form of mimicry is the theatre or the carnival, the institutional form being love of uniforms and ceremonial, the corruption appearing as feelings of alienation and depersonalisation. Finally the cultural form of the pursuit of vertigo is mountain climbing, sport involving speed, etc.; the institutional form is found in professions requiring control of vertigo (like that of the steeple-jack); the corrupt form is the use of alcohol and drugs.

If there has been a movement towards the corruption of games, is it possible to blame these changes upon Freud? Huizinga warns against this. 'Is it so certain that the new schools of society are not being led astray by the frivolous and facile use of Freudian terminology at the hands of competents and incompetents alike?' Indeed no: if anything the certainty lies in the other direction.

What is true of psychoanalysis is true of behaviourism. It is true that many of its practitioners talk of manipulating men as if they were machines; it is true, also, that some of their more extreme forms of 'treatment' of the perverted are abhorrent to those who do not share their faith; but these manifestations are perversions of a viewpoint which, with its concern for personal conduct and interpersonal behaviour, is essentially humane.

The views of McLuhan and the writings of certain contemporary novelists may similarly be regarded as perversions of the humane idea that we should study the world as we experience it rather than interpret it in terms of metaphysical significance: they are perversions to the extent that they deny the existence of reality behind surface appearances, and refuse to interpret phenomena symbolically. In their denial of all reality except superficial appearance they are in line with Berkeley rather than Hume, but it is Berkeley without God. The poet who wrote of 'the God-appointed Berkeley, who made all things a dream' could hardly have foreseen that his dream would become our nightmare.

The reaction against the more extreme statements of the behaviourists has led to a revival of interest in phenomenology, i.e., the attempt to understand the individual from his own viewpoint. In 1964 the proceedings of a symposium on *Behaviourism and Phenomenology* were published, edited by Wann, the contributors to which included D. T. Campbell. More recently Campbell has contributed a paper on phenomenology to Mischel's *Human Action* symposium. The view expressed by Campbell is that behaviourism of the Hull type is outmoded, and that philosophers of science today favour the approach of Tolman (see Broadbent, 1961, for a discussion of these viewpoints) or of Miller, Galanter and Pribram. As Koestler (1967) points out, people are always saying that behaviourism is dead, but this dead horse continues to pull the psychological cart; certainly the sophistication of Campbell is counterbalanced by the naivety of Skinner. Be that as it may the fact is that one may approach the study of human behaviour either from the observation of responses to stimuli or from an attempt to understand the behaver's interpretation of the stimuli. It is certainly more convenient to study overt behaviour than to speculate on the meaning that stimuli have for the person whom they stimulate, but neither approach has priority as a basis for epistemology. For this reason Campbell and others would like to see phenomenology and behaviourism united, but the attempt to unite them regrettably involves recourse to word-spinning and to proposals such as the following: 'conscious experience . . . is isomorphic to meaningful response' and 'meaningful conscious experience is isomorphic to the neural brain stream . . .' and so on. 'Isomorphic' literally means 'having the same shape'. To talk of experience 'having the same shape as' nerve impulses is to extend the meanings of terms rather in the way in which Chomsky accuses Skinner of extending behaviouristic terminology. Essentially such formulations mean no more than that there is a correlation between certain experiences and certain brain patterns, which is, for the most part, far from being proved. Feigl deals with this situation by distinguishing meaning from reference. For instance if I say 'Queen Elizabeth II is Queen of England' the terms 'Queen Elizabeth II' and 'Queen of England' *refer* to the same person, but they do not *mean* the same thing. Similarly neurophysiological terms and phenomenological terms have identical *referents* but differ in *meaning*, i.e., 'in the modes of confirmation of statements confirming them' (see Chapter 12 for a discussion of meaning as mode of verification). However, to discuss this further would involve us too deeply in consideration of the irresolvable mind-body problem.

Whatever the ultimate direction of advance, one thing seems clear. So long as psychologists and others continue to formulate their findings and theories in terms that appear to deny the symbolic significance of things and events, there will be vehement objections from those who see in symbolisation the essence of conscious awareness.

It should not surprise us to find that an age in which symbolism is devalued is one in which the function of play is also disturbed. In the first place, the behaviourists whose treatment of language implicitly denies its symbolic significance also deny the usefulness of the concept of play, regarding the term 'play' as loosely applicable to behaviour that could be more rigidly described in terms describing features of overt behaviour (Schlosberg).[1] In the second place, play and symbolism have the same roots; both originate in man's attempts to come to terms with the environment. In Chapter 5 we cited Piaget's example of the little girl opening her mouth whilst trying to force a chain into a matchbox that was too small to accept it; the little girl was imitating a feature of the environment, and her open mouth was symbolic of the matchbox that was causing her such difficulty. We shall see in Chapter 10 that Piaget regards adaptation to the environment as a balance between accommodation (modifying one's schemes of actions and images to take account of environmental novelties) and assimilation (accepting new environmental features into already developed schemes). In the symbolic play of the young child, as in play generally, assimilation is dominant. One attempts, in play and other fantasy, to manipulate reality for one's own ends. Strictly speaking we are concerned here with only one sort of play, pure or *ludic* play, which is peculiar to man, rather than the boisterous mock fighting that is a preparation for adult life, which children share with animals. (For a recent survey of the psychology of play see Millar. For Piaget's views see Piaget and Inhelder, ch. 3.) Ludic play and symbolism are among the defining characteristics of humanity and may well be the foundations upon which his rationality is built. When these are under attack the house of reason itself is threatened with collapse.

[1] Schlosberg argues that 'playing' is not in the same logical category as running, leaping, biting, etc., which animals exhibit in their play. Whilst this is correct, it does not follow that an analysis in terms of observable behaviour would account for play, any more than a description of a man laughing and clapping is an adequate account of his 'enjoying' himself.

PART TWO
Language and Thinking

7

REASONING AND PROBLEM-SOLVING

In Chapter 1 we offered a preliminary definition of thinking as symbolic problem-solving. Problem-solving is a form of reasoning, but not all reasoning is problem-solving. For instance it is held to be characteristic of a genius that he sees what problems there are to be solved, not that he necessarily solves them; in other words the study of thinking must take account of originality in reasoning. In this chapter and the next we shall examine some theories of thinking to see how well they account for known facts (these chapters do not pretend to be an exhaustive survey, but are limited to a discussion of major themes: the reader wishing to obtain a more complete picture is referred to the selections of readings made by Duncan, Ray, and Wason and Johnson-Laird).

The two chief theories of thinking expounded by experimental psychologists come from the behaviourist and the gestalt psychologists respectively. We shall examine the behaviourist account first. This explanation of thinking, first expounded by Hull, was developed by Osgood, and has been given its most recent formulation by Maltzman. The behaviourist regards the learning process as the strengthening of responses to stimuli by the medium of reinforcement. The learning factor is symbolised by H for 'habit', and the efficiency of learning may be thought of in terms of the strength of the habit. A habit is seldom a single response to a single stimulus, as the same response may occur to more than one stimulus. By way of illustration we may consider the question of sexual arousal, not so much for its intrinsic interest as because Hullian learning principles have been widely applied by clinical psychologists in this sphere. A man may be aroused by the presence of a woman, a photo of a woman, or the sight of women's clothing. So long as he is more aroused by the woman than by the other stimuli we can say that the stimuli are in a correct hierarchical order. If not, the clinical pscyhologist must attempt to modify the hierarchy. Now let us consider the response. A man who is sexually roused may desire normal intercourse or some perversion. So long as the desire for intercourse is dominant, then his response hierarchy is satisfactory; if not, it must be altered by the clinician.

Now let us represent this in terms of symbols. In Fig. 7:1 we see that simuli S_1, S_2, S_3 may all arouse responses R_1, R_2, R_3. The stimulus hierarchy is said to be 'convergent', the response hierarchy to be 'divergent'. All the stimuli and responses together form a 'habit family hierarchy'. All behaviour may be thought of as composed of interlocking habit family hierarchies.

Stimuli need not be physically present to have an effect on an individual. He may simply have to think about them to become

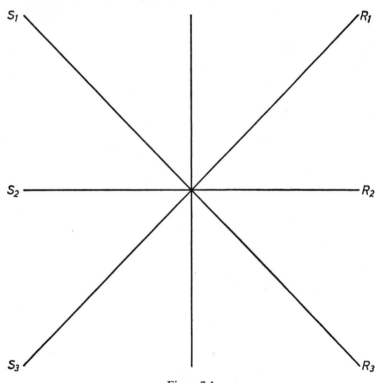

Figure 7:1
A simple habit family hierarchy.

aroused. The idea in his head may be thought of as a fractional stimulus, and his arousal as a fractional response. Becoming aroused by an idea is called 'fractional anticipatory goal response', and is symbolised as r_{ga}–s_{ga}. The fractional anticipatory goal response links together all the stimuli for the individual so that eliminating the stimulating effect of one will have the effect of eliminating the stimulating effect of the others, by a process of generalisation mediated by the fractional anticipatory goal response. This creates considerable problems for the clinician, but leads to verifiable predictions for psychologists who developed this theory from the study of rats.

Let us take our picture a little further, taking this time an example from the everyday fact of eating. If I am hungry I have an internal drive state that sets off some activity in search of food. If a colleague knocks on my door and suggests going to lunch, I may go even if I am not hungry. Here then are two stimuli, which we shall call S_A and S_B. In the normal course of events I may go to lunch at a regular time, not because I am hungry or because someone invites me but because I know that I can get food and companionship at that hour, so at that time my mind starts wandering from my work. This is my fractional anticipatory goal response. On arriving at the refectory I shall probably first visit the bar, where I may drink sherry (R_1) or madeira (R_2). Finishing the drink will increase my desire to eat, so I may symbolise the stimulus caused by the sherry as S_1 and that caused by the madeira as S_2. I now go to eat, and since eating was my original goal, I can represent the response of eating as R_G. Fig. 7:2 represents the total situation.

How does this apply to thinking? To answer that question we must picture a situation in which S_A may set off a divergent response

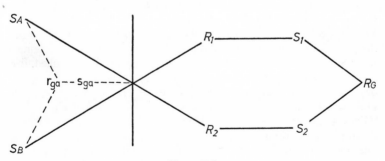

Figure 7:2
A complex habit family hierarchy.

hierarchy R_1, R_2 etc; and S_B may set off another divergent hierarchy R'_1, R'_2 etc. Let us say that R_1, R_2 lead to goal R_{GA}, and that R'_1, R'_2 lead to R_{GB}. We have the situation pictured in Fig. 7:3.

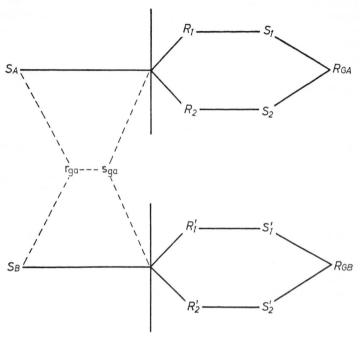

Figure 7:3
A compound habit family hierarchy.

We see from Fig. 7:3 that the fractional anticipatory goal response r_{ga}–s_{ga} may cause S_A to set off responses R_1 or R_2, and may cause S_B to set off R^1_1 or R^1_2. Whether or not this happens depends upon the probability that a response will be reinforced. If the experimenter so arranges conditions that the obvious path to a goal is blocked, the subject may try another path, and possibly arrive at another goal, one that he may not have foreseen. Let us take an example from Duncker. Duncker set his subjects the following problem to solve: 'Given a patient with an inoperable stomach tumour, and rays which destroy organic tissue at sufficient intensity, by what procedure can one free him of the tumour by these rays and at the same time avoid destroying the healthy tissue which surrounds it?'

The obvious way to destroy the tumour, by directing a strong beam of rays at it, is not permissible, as this would destroy the intervening healthy tissue. The correct solution, which in experiments involving such problems usually appears after a number of unacceptable solutions have been rejected, is to send weak rays from different directions to converge upon the tumour, so that only at the point of convergence is the intensity sufficient to destroy tissue. The behaviourist explanation is that the habitual responses, leading as they do to unacceptable solutions, are not reinforced, so the subjects must seek new solutions. The correct response must have been in their repertoire, but they had not linked it to the problem situation until, under the compulsion to find a solution they had realised that it was appropriate. The correct response was linked to the stimulus (the problem situation) by the fractional anticipatory goal response. This therefore mediated the appearance of the correct solution, and we are entitled to call it a 'mediating response'.

Ingenious though this explanation is, there is something unsatisfactory about it. If responses are linked to stimuli by reinforcement, we should expect the new response to require a number of reinforcements before it is established, but typically this is not so. (For another aspect of the same criticism see Chapter 12.) Once the solution has been seen it is usually remembered, because the subject's cognitive grasp of the situation has been altered. We say that he has 'insight', i.e., that he has 'seen' the problem in a new way. This is the view of the gestalt psychologists, to which school Duncker belongs. Duncker sums up his view of problem-solving as follows: 'Every solution consists in some alterations of the given situation. But not only this or that in the situation is changed, i.e., not only such alterations take place as one would have to mention in a simple commonsense description; over and beyond this the *psychological structure of the situation* as a *whole* or of certain significant parts is changed. Such alterations are called restructurations.'

Another psychologist whose work exemplifies the gestalt view is Wertheimer (1950), who is concerned to show that in cases of productive thinking there is a reorganisation of the cognitive field, which enables us to see new principles of belonging. He illustrates this by reference to a familar type of syllogism:

> All men are mortal
> Socrates is a man
> Therefore Socrates is mortal.

We are able to draw the conclusion that Socrates is mortal because we know that Socrates is a man, and that every member of the class *man* is mortal. Much of our productive thinking involves seeing to which class a particular instance belongs, so that we may draw relevant conclusions.

Here are two examples from geometry. In Fig. 7:4 the problem is to find the total area of the square plus parallelogram. The problem is readily solved if we see that we have two triangles as indicated in Fig. 7:5:

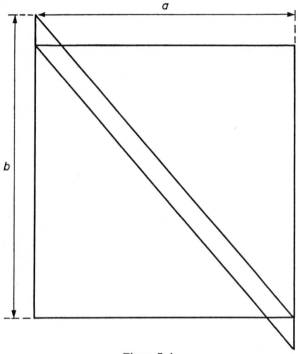

Figure 7:4
Wertheimer's square and parallelogram problem.

In Fig. 7:6 the problem is to find the area of the isosceles triangle of side s, given that the angle between the sides is $90°$. Fig. 7:7 shows that the simplest way to solve the problem is to visualise the triangle as tipped on its side. The area $= \frac{1}{2}(b \times h) = s^2/2$. The line a in Fig. 7:6 helps to divert attention away from the direction of the solution.

The behaviourist and gestalt views of problem-solving may seem to be alternatives. In fact the picture is a little more complicated than that. We said that, once a response has been gained by insight it does not require reinforcement, but there are cases in which insight

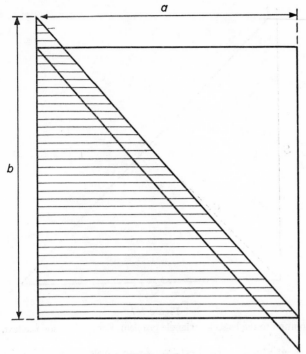

Figure 7:5
Solution to the square and parallelogram problem.

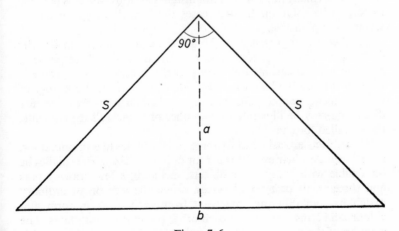

Figure 7:6
Wertheimer's isosceles triangle problem. For explanation see text.

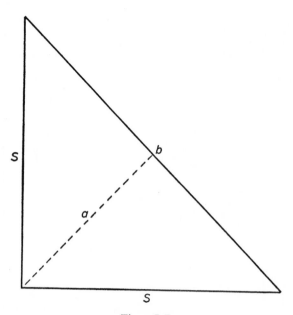

Figure 7:7

Solution to the isosceles triangle problem. For explanation see text.

develops gradually, the best-known examples being the familiar metal puzzles of the twisted nails variety. Often one needs to solve such puzzles many times before full insight develops, and it is possible to forget the solution. In such cases the behaviourist explanation seems more plausible.

Another question that must be asked in this connection is: why do people persist in wrong solutions? If a particular response is right on most occasions but wrong in the context of the problem, then once more the behaviourist account in terms of the history of reinforcement seems plausible. The phenomenon that we are discussing may be illustrated by another of Duncker's experiments, the so-called 'box problem'.

The subjects are asked to fix three small candles to a smooth door, at the height of their eyes (it is a door of normal size). The candles lie on a table with many other objects, including a few drawing pins and three small pasteboard boxes, about the size of an ordinary matchbox, but differing somewhat from each other in form and colour, and lying not next to each other but in different places. The solution of the problem is to fasten the three boxes to the door with drawing pins. The boxes will then serve as platforms for the candles.

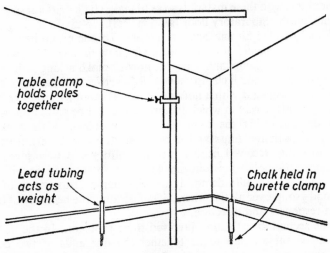

THE MATERIAL

Burette clamps   Table clamp   Pieces of chalk

Coils of wire   Lead tubing

Poles

THE SOLUTION

Table clamp holds poles together

Lead tubing acts as weight

Chalk held in burette clamp

Figure 7:8
Maier's pendulum problem.

For half the subjects the boxes were filled with matches, drawing pins, and small candles, for the other half they were empty. The subjects for whom the boxes were filled found the task more difficult to solve because they had it fixed in their minds that these boxes were containers, and they had difficulty in visualising them as platforms for candles. Duncker describes this phenomenon as 'functional fixedness'.

Other investigators whose work revealed this phenomenon include Maier (1930, 1931, 1933) and Luchins. The work of these investigators is well known, and need be described only briefly (for a detailed account of Maier's work, see Crafts *et al.* and Osgood).

Maier's basic thesis was that successful solution of a problem requires not only the selection of appropriate responses from the organism's repertoire but also the right approach or *direction*. Without the right direction one cannot organise the part-responses in such a way as to get the solution. To demonstrate this point of view Maier carried out three investigations. In one investigation the subjects were given four poles, a number of clamps, lengths of wire, pieces of chalk, and lead tubing. They were asked to make two pendulums with these materials so as to make chalk marks at specified points on the laboratory floor (see Fig. 7:8).

Maier divided his subjects into groups. To one group he demonstrated the elements of the problem, viz., how to make a plumb line from a cord, a clamp, and a pencil; how to make a long pole given two short poles and a clamp; how to fix a vertical bar against a door jamb by wedging it with a horizontal bar. To another group he gave hints about the way in which the problem could be solved but without demonstrating the elements of the problem. A third group received both the hints and a demonstration of the elements. A fourth group received neither, whilst a fifth group were given the demonstrations but not told that they had anything to do with the problem. The results demonstrated the marked superiority of the second group over all the others, demonstrating the necessity of both part-responses and direction.

The second investigation involved three problems. In the first of these the subject had to tie together the free ends of two cords hanging from the ceiling to the floor, the two cords being too far apart to enable one to be reached whilst the other was held. (The solution was to tie a pair of pliers to one cord and swing it whilst holding the other.) In the second the subject had to make a stable hatrack from two poles and a clamp (see Fig. 7:9, which is self-explanatory). The third problem was to blow out a lighted candle eight feet away, given certain materials (see Fig. 7:10). This investigation concerned the possibility that the wrong direction might *prevent* the appearance of the correct solution. To investigate this possibility Maier divided his subjects into two groups, one of which worked at the problem without help, the other receiving a preliminary talk on the advisability of keeping the mind open to new ideas. The group receiving this talk achieved greater success than the other, confirming Maier's view.

The third investigation concerned the fact that people often solve a problem without being able to say how they have done it. To find out why this was so Maier used again the two-cord problem employed in the second investigation. Subjects who failed to solve the problem in a certain time were given a 'hint', i.e., the experimenter brushed past the string apparently accidentally, starting it swinging. (If this hint failed they were handed the pair of pliers two minutes later and told that they could solve the problem by using that tool.

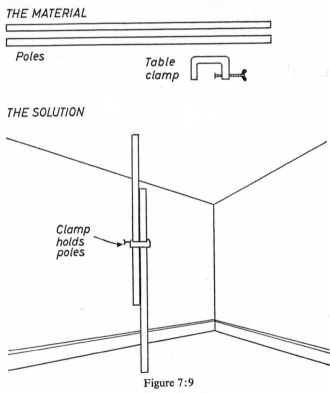

Figure 7:9
Maier's hatrack problem.

THE MATERIAL

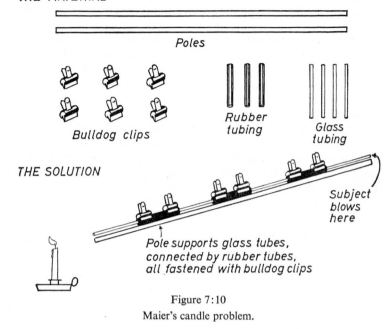

Poles

Bulldog clips

Rubber tubing

Glass tubing

THE SOLUTION

Subject blows here

Pole supports glass tubes, connected by rubber tubes, all fastened with bulldog clips

Figure 7:10
Maier's candle problem.

Few subjects needed the second hint.) Most subjects who solved the problem after the first hint denied being aware of receiving a hint, although they had worked at the problem for 10 minutes before the hint without success, but solved it in an average time of 42 seconds after the hint.

These investigations suggest that both the gestalt and the behaviourist explanations of problem-solving are appropriate, though the appropriateness of one or the other depends upon the problem.

Luchins's famous experiment can be described more briefly. The type of problem set can be stated as follows. Given three jars of stated capacities, obtain a specified volume of water, without guessing at partial quantities, i.e., one must fill a jar to the brim in order to be sure of obtaining the stated amount – one cannot for instance 'half-fill' as there is no indication of the half-way mark.

For instance: given jars of 21, 127, and 3 pints capacities respectively, obtain 100 pints. The solution is to fill the 127 pint jar. From this one fills the 21 pint jar, leaving 106 pints in the largest jar. One empties 3 pints into the 3 pint jar, throws this away and pours a further 3 pints into it. This leaves 100 pints in the largest jar.

Here is another example. Given jars of 26, 76, and 126 pints capacities, obtain 24 pints. There are two solutions to this.

1. Fill the 126 pint jar and pour 76 pints from this into the 76 pint jar leaving 50 pints. Pour 26 into the smallest jar, leaving 24.

2. Fill the 76 pint jar, pour 26 into the smallest jar, empty this and repeat.

Thus, one solution involves use of all three jars, the other involves only two.

The question that Luchins set out to solve experimentally was as follows: if subjects had experience only of problems that required three jars for their solution, would they overlook a two-jar solution when they encountered a problem that could be solved in this way? To answer this question Luchins had two groups.

1. The experimental group worked at problems that required three jars for their solution.

2. The control group worked at a mixture of problems, some of which could only be solved by the use of all three jars, others being soluble only if two jars alone were used, ignoring the third.

After solving these problems, both groups were given a further set of problems (the same set for both groups). All of those were soluble using either all three jars or two alone, the two-jar solution being frequently simpler. Luchins found that a smaller number of the experimental group chose the simpler solutions than was the case for the control group. He explained this by saying that the experimental situation had induced a *set* or *Einstellung* to approach the problems in one way rather than another.

In later experiments Luchins and Luchins investigated the possibility that actual handling of jars might make the problems less abstract, thus reducing the Einstellung effect. Surprisingly this was not so, as some subjects continued to regard the problems as abstractions rather than concrete problems. Thus in the problem: given jars of capacities 5 quarts, 25 quarts, and 10 quarts, obtain 0 quarts, some subjects solved the problem as $25-5-(2\times10)=0$. These subjects comprised fifty per cent of a class of college students. Such results should make us cautious when interpreting empirical investigations of thinking, as it seems unlikely that anyone would behave like this in real life.

So far in this chapter we have presented two views of thinking: the behaviourist view that thinking is an activity requiring the reinforcement of correct responses, the gestalt view that, when presented with a problem, the mind actively seeks to reorganise the material, in order to give it significance (the law of Prägnanz). A third view is associated with Sir Frederick Bartlett, namely that thinking is a form of skill. Inasmuch as a skill is an integrated activity, requiring practice as well as natural talent, Bartlett's view falls somewhere between the behaviourist and gestalt views.

What is the nature of this skill? Bartlett regards it as, in essence, the filling up of gaps in evidence. He distinguishes 'thinking within closed systems' from 'adventurous thinking'. In adventurous or creative thinking, the individual must discover for himself gaps in evidence of which other people have not previously been aware: this is difficult to demonstrate, so we may consider examples from the field of thinking within closed systems. Bartlett reports experiments to demonstrate that gaps may be filled in one of three ways: interpolation, extrapolation, and the unmasking of evidence in disguise.

Interpolation

1. Given: 1   17

'Take 1 as the first and 17 as the last number and fill up the gap between them in any way that seems to be indicated.' This problem is readily solved, the commonest solutions according to Bartlett being 3, 5, 7, 9, 11, 13, 15 (i.e., the odd numbers); 2, 3, 4, etc. (all the numbers); and 9 (the midpoint). The present author has found 3, 5, 7, 11, 13 (i.e., the prime numbers) to be commoner than fractionation by the number 9.

2. Given: *A, BY,*   *HORRIBLE*
'Look at the terminal words and then fill up the gap in any way that you think to be indicated.' Again this is readily solved, and most subjects (at least at the undergraduate level) see that the direction of the change is two-directional, so that the third word must have three letters beginning with *C* (e.g., cat); the next must have four letters beginning with *D* (e.g., door).

Extrapolation

1. Given the following:

A, GATE, NO, I, DUTY, IN, CAT,
BO, EAR, O, TRAVEL, ERASE, BOTH
GET, HO, FATE

ERASE
FATE

The subject is instructed 'From the group of words at the top, complete the vertical arrangement indicated by the two words "erase" and "fate", taking "erase" as the middle word in the problem. Not all the words given need be used.'

Once more we have a two-directional change, the solution being as follows:

```
                A
            B       O
        C       A       T
    D       U       T       Y
E       R       A       S       E
    F       A       T       E
        G       E       T
            H       O
                I
```

According to Bartlett only about two people in a hundred selected at random achieve this solution.

2. Given the following:

$$1234: \qquad 2134: \qquad 2143$$

'Continue the change until an arrangement has been reached where it seems "natural" or "sensible" to stop.'

The commonest continuations are as follows:

1234	:	2134	:	2143	2413, 4213, 4231, 4321
1234	:	2134	:	2143	1243, 1234

In the first continuation the pairs of numbers are varied in turn until the original sequence is reversed. In the second the argument is that the first two have been reversed, then the second two. If one repeats the operation one returns to the starting point.

Evidence in disguise

In the following sum letters stand for digits.

$$DONALD$$
$$+GERALD$$
$$\overline{}$$
$$=ROBERT$$

$D=5$; every digit from 1 to 0 is represented; no letter stands for more than one digit. The problem is to substitute digits for letters to make an arithmetical sum. The problem will be left for the reader's amusement, but as a clue we may say that one difficulty is caused by the sum $O+E=O$. Until this is overcome the problem is insoluble:

normally one solves a sum from right to left, but in this case the left side must be solved first.

Ingenious though Bartlett's demonstrations are they seem a little artificial and strained. One has the impression that the tasks were invented to illustrate a thesis arrived at on *a priori* grounds rather than that the thesis was the conclusion from experimental studies. Unfortunately the same is true of the experiments of the behaviourists and the gestalt psychologists. This is not necessarily an objection as, if a thesis is adequate, it does not matter how it originated. However, writers in this field often give the impression that their work is the fruit of empirical study, and the experiments that they quote often disguise the fact that they are writing from predetermined theoretical positions.

If what we have said is true of work on problem-solving, it is even truer of the work on original thinking, which we shall consider in the next chapter.

8

INTELLIGENCE AND CREATIVITY

The word 'intelligence' is so widely used today that one is tempted to suppose it to be a term of great antiquity. On the contrary, Sir Cyril Burt (1967, 1968) has pointed out that it was coined in the early years of this century by workers interested in general mental ability.

'Creativity' is an older term, but its use in psychology is more recent than that of 'intelligence'. Within the last decade psychologists have sought to establish a general intellectual dimension, independent of intelligence, but of the same order of importance. The best-known example of research in this field is that of Getzels and Jackson. The research has tried to show, by means of correlation analysis, that performance on tests of creativity involves a set of abilities different from those required for success on intelligence tests.

The children of the Getzels and Jackson study were drawn from a private school in the Chicago area. This was a highly selected population, as the mean IQ of the school (on Stanford–Binet type tests) was 132, with an s.d. of 15.[1] The ages of the children ranged from 11 to 18.

All children in the school were given tests of creativity, these tests being as follows:

1. Word association – to find as many definitions as possible to common words.
2. Uses for things – to find as many uses as possible for an object such as a brick.
3. Hidden shapes – finding simple geometric patterns incorporated in complex patterns.
4. Fables – providing three endings to a brief story; 'moralistic', 'humorous', and 'sad'.

[1] i.e., 68 per cent of the children had IQs between 132 ± 15.

5. Made-up problems – how many problems can be constructed from a page of numerical data.

These tests were found to distinguish clearly between different modes of thinking. For instance, to the word 'bolt', many students would think only of a bolt on a door, or the verb 'to bolt'. Few would think of 'a bolt of cloth'. Similarly many would be able to think of using a brick for building, hammering, filling a hole, etc. Few would think of scooping a hollow in the brick and using it as an ashtray. Further, on the fables test, students differed in the amount of imagination displayed in thinking of endings.

These differences in thinking were not paralleled by differences in intelligence; many of the most intelligent students (i.e., those who scored most highly on tests of intelligence) did poorly on the tests of creativity; whereas some scoring most highly on the creativity tests did relatively poorly on the intelligence tests. This was not always so, of course; some students did relatively well on both intelligence and creativity tests, others relatively poorly on both. For the purposes of this study, such students (i.e., those whose intelligence scores were in line with their creativity scores) were excluded from consideration, as Getzels and Jackson were concerned with *differences* in cognitive functioning.

Therefore the investigators distinguished two groups as follows:

1. *High Creativity Group* – students in the top 20 per cent on creativity measures but below the top 20 per cent in IQ (26 altogether – 15 boys, 11 girls).

2. *High Intelligence Group* – students in the top 20 per cent in intelligence but below the top 20 per cent on creativity measures (28 altogether – 17 boys, 11 girls).

An independent approach by Guilford has distinguished *convergent* from *divergent* thinking. Convergent thinking efficiently seeks solutions to problems in a conventional manner and is assessed by intelligence tests, whereas divergent thinking not only finds novel solutions but also recognises problems not recognised by others. This distinction is akin to Bartlett's distinction between 'thinking within closed systems' and 'adventurous thinking'. Some people have sought to identify convergent thinking with a preference for science and divergent with preference for the humanities, but whilst there may be some such correlation amongst school children (Hudson) there is no evidence that the highest intellects in science and the humanities can be dichotomised in this way.

Most of the work on different modes of employing the intellect has been performed in the past ten years, since the appearance of Getzels and Jackson's book, but some earlier studies by Witkin are relevant. These studies were based not on problem-solving but on perception.

When we perceive objects and events we make judgements about the stimuli that impinge upon us. For this reason perception is seldom entirely objective, but is influenced by our habitual ways of thinking. In 1949 Witkin systematically investigated problems of the perception of the vertical in space, research that was in 1954 extended by Witkin and his associates to a study of the relations between perception and personality.

One of the perceptual tasks studied was the ability to perceive simple figures embedded in complex designs; another was more elaborate. In this case the subject was seated in a chair in a room; both chair and room could be tilted to a required angle. The subject was required to adjust either room or chair (with himself in it) to a vertical position. Various confusing visual cues could be introduced, and the task was elaborated to include adjustment of a luminous rod in a luminous frame.

Adjustment of the body (in the chair) requires the subject to ignore the distracting visual cues, which constitute the perceptual field in which the body is situated: adjustment of the room, as distinct from the body, requires the subject to respond to the perceptual field. According to their customary modes of response, subjects were dubbed 'field-dependent' or 'field-independent'.

Field-dependent persons, as defined by these experiments, were found to be passive in dealing with the environment, fearful of their own impulses, and to have an unclear picture of their own size and shape. The field-independent subjects, on the other hand, were more active in their relation with the environment, and found to have better control of their own impulses, and to have a mature body-image. These personality characteristics were assessed by a number of tests, including the Rorschach Ink Blot Test, in which the subject has to say what a standard series of meaningless shapes reminds him of; Murray's Thematic Apperception Test, in which the subject is required to tell stories about a standard set of ambiguous pictures; and by interviews.

Extensive studies found that the attitudes revealed by the experiments, tests, and interviews were sufficiently consistent in a given individual to permit one to talk of his 'cognitive style'. The field-independent person was said to have an 'analytical' style, whereas the field-dependent individual could be described as having a 'global' style. The analytical thinker, being more able to separate parts from wholes, is more likely to be creative than the global thinker. However, no convincing evidence has linked these styles with the divergent/convergent distinction mentioned above.

Whilst it would be inappropriate in a book on language and thinking to deal at any length with these studies of perception and personality, one or two general points are of interest. In the first place more women than men are field-dependent in the experimental situation and global in cognitive style: this is consistent with the finding that fewer women than men are found in creative occupations. However, women are much less consistent in their responses to the experimental situation than are men. The second point concerns child development. In situations requiring the subject to adjust a rod, or his body, to the vertical, also in tasks involving embedded figures, perception is greatly influenced by the surrounding field in the case of children under 10; between 10 and 12 the influence of the field decreases markedly; after 12 there are few changes in suscepti- bility to field influence until the age of 15 to 17. After 17 there is a reversal of this tendency, so that adults are more susceptible to the perceptual field than are children, but this reversal is more marked for men than for women; moreover this reversal begins earlier for girls than for boys (on average age 15 as opposed to age 17).

There are some methodological weaknesses in this study. In particular the fact that personality was assessed by tests involving perception (Rorschach and TAT) constitutes an objection in a study purporting to show the relations between perception and personality. Moreover all tests of personality that depend upon the interpretation of the subjects' responses to ambiguous stimuli (the so-called 'pro- jective' tests) are notoriously unreliable; interviews are even more so. For this reason one cannot feel very confident that the cognitive styles that have been identified rest upon a convincing body of empirical evidence.

Whereas Witkin's work relied upon finding correlations between performances on perceptual tasks, personality tests, and cognitive problems, the work of Getzels and Jackson and of Wallach and Kogan rests upon analysis of correlations between scores on different types of cognitive task. Let us consider what would be necessary to establish, by correlation analysis, the existence of independent intellectual dimensions. We should require there to be two sets of tests, each satisfying the requirements of reliability and validity.[1] In the case of intelligence these tests exist, as the con-

[1] Briefly 'reliability' refers to the consistency with which a test gives the same result on different occasions. 'Validity' refers to the success with which a test measures what it claims to measure.

ventional 'intelligence tests'. Getzels and Jackson, in their research, were obliged to construct their own tests of creativity. As Burt, reviewing their work, pointed out, they did not establish the reliability of their tests.

The sorts of tests employed in creativity measurement inevitably involve an element of subjective judgement on the tester's part. Such tests were originally incorporated in intelligence tests, but were dropped because of their low reliabilities. Unfortunately the requirements of reliability are sometimes incompatible with those of validity. Let us suppose that the criterion against which intelligence tests are to be validated is academic success. It may be that 75 per cent of successful pupils succeed academically because they possess certain abilities that are unambiguously measurable, but that the remainder succeed because of abilities that are not easily measured. If the items that tap the abilities of the minority are dropped because of their low reliabilities, then 25 per cent of the pupils will make relatively low scores but still succeed academically. The temptation is to say that they have succeeded despite low intelligence, whereas the true situation is that the test has failed to measure their intelligence, though it has succeeded with the majority.

The reason why such a situation may arise is that any criterion against which an intelligence test is likely to be validated (be it academic success or anything else) will inevitably be very complex because intelligence is a concept of great complexity. There has been much debate in the history of psychology about the nature of intelligence, and three main views may be distinguished.

1. Intelligence consists of a general factor and a number of specific factors.
2. It comprises group factors (e.g., verbal comprehension, verbal fluency, numerical ability, spatial ability, and reasoning).
3. There is both a general factor and group factors.

The generally held view today is that whether group factors emerge, or even whether a general factor emerges, is a function of how test items are put together in the construction of a test.

The implications of what we have said for the intelligence creativity controversy are as follows. Let us suppose people who succeed on creativity tests to have a set of abilities C, and those who succeed on intelligence tests to have a set of abilities I. If C and I overlap we shall have the situation shown in Fig. 8:1. The individuals in the shaded portion will be high on both intelligence and creativity.

This may be the situation explored by Getzels and Jackson, although the situation they claimed to be exploring is represented by

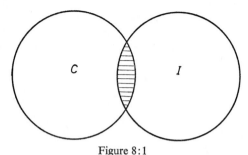

Figure 8:1

Overlapping of abilities tapped by tests of creativity and of intelligence.

Fig. 8:2. We should note that they deliberately ignored the individuals in the shaded portion. Furthermore they had no individuals *low* on *both* creativity and intelligence, because they studied a group specially selected for high intelligence.

Other investigators have made more general studies, and their findings, along with those of Getzels and Jackson, are discussed by Wallach and Kogan. They find that the inter-correlations among the creativity measures are either not significant (suggesting that creativity

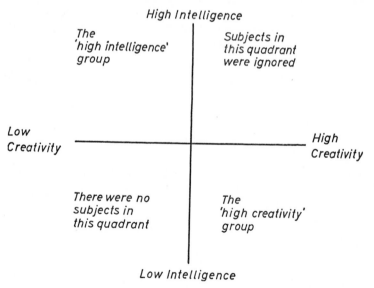

Figure 8:2

The situation investigated by Getzels and Jackson.

is not a unitary dimension); or that they are no higher than their correlation with IQ (suggesting that creativity is not a separate dimension from intelligence).

This finding leads them to ask whether there is no dimension of creativity, or whether previous investigators have failed to assess it. They conclude that the latter is true, and that new tests are required.

Let us break off to consider the question of validity. Undoubtedly individuals do vary in creativity, if by creativity we mean the capacity to invent something that was not previously in existence, whether it be a work of art, a scientific or mathematical theory or a new conceptualisation of existing data. Precisely what is involved in creating is, and has long been, a matter of debate. Koestler, in *The Act of Creation*, uses the joke as the paradigm of a creation, because the joke makes us laugh by juxtaposing two previously unrelated ideas, and revealing their essential relation. In much the same way, a creative genius will show the essential relation between previously unrelated sets of ideas, and will make of them an idea that is new because, although its elements are old, their logical juxtaposition makes of them something else, something that exists in its own right. An essential condition of creativity as thus conceived would be the rapid and profuse production of ideas, from which combinations might arise.

Not everyone will accept this analysis of what is involved in creating but Koestler's analysis may be taken to illustrate an important difficulty in the field of creativity measurement, namely that what one regards as an adequate measure depends on how one conceptualises creativity. The same difficulty arises with regard to intelligence testing as well, but the problem here has been largely evaded by the expedient of constructing tests that correlate with narrowly defined criteria. Thus we have tests of academic aptitude, of numerical aptitude, of secretarial aptitude, and so on. Even the so-called 'intelligence scales' choose, as their validation criteria, something narrower than their constructors' conceptualisations of intelligence. Wechsler, for instance, admits that his tests are really measures of *intellectual* ability, but maintains that this is the best measure of intelligence, which includes social ability. Whether Wechsler's tests really measure intellectual ability is, of course, partly what the intelligence/creativity debate is about.

In the field of creativity it is very difficult to see what we are going to regard as an appropriate validation criterion. Are we trying to pick out, when young, the individuals who will later be most likely to create something original? If so, our aim is very restricted, because so few people do this. Are we trying to do something less ambitious, for instance to distinguish rigid from less rigid personalities? If so we have tests for this already, namely personality tests (see Rokeach). Are we trying to increase the validity of tests of mental ability? If so, we shall finish with tests of low internal consistency, for the reason mentioned above. It is against the background of this discussion that we have to consider Wallach and Kogan's conceptualisation of creativity.

They argue that, if subjects are asked to produce associative responses of a given type (e.g., the ways in which different objects are similar), these subjects will differ in the *number* and *uniqueness* of the responses produced and that these measures will be related, as will be described later. Obviously the responses must be in their repertoire in order to be produced at all, and so individuals of different cognitive abilities may differ in their response behaviour simply because they cannot *store* the same number of associations. A safeguard against this possibility is to compare individuals of the same IQ level, as these will presumably be of the same level of cognitive ability. If individuals of the same IQ nevertheless differ in the number and uniqueness of the associations that they produce, then the independence of creativity and intelligence will have been demonstrated.

Wallach and Kogan suggest that noncreative individuals will produce only stereotyped associates, and may well produce them quickly. The creative individual may also begin by producing stereotyped responses, though possibly not as many as the noncreative, but will continue responding, with unique associations, after the noncreative individual has stopped. The implication is that a timed test is not appropriate for measuring creativity.

One other aspect of the problem is that creative individuals often refer to a feeling of play in their creative activity. Consequently, a test situation, which is explicitly concerned with evaluation rather than play, is not appropriate for measuring creativity.

Some investigators have suggested that, because individuals differ in their preference for the verbal or the visual mode, and may produce more associations in one way than the other, both should be sampled. However, if creativity is a unitary dimension, as is argued, the mode of presentation should not affect the associative ability of the subjects. Wallach and Kogan therefore presented visual and verbal measures to test their correlation.

All measures were administered by two woman researchers, familiar to the children, in the form of games. Two group measures of aptitude and attainment were part of the school's routine assessment programme; three individual measures were administered last in sequence by the researchers. These were WISC[1] Vocabulary, Block Design, and Picture Arrangement. The creativity tests were administered before these in order to avoid contamination of the creativity measures by the strain of the evaluative intelligence tests.

There were 151 children (70 boys and 81 girls), predominantly of middle-class parents, of average 10 years 7·60 months (s.d. 5·42 months). The five creativity measures were as follows:

Instances
'In this game I am going to tell you something and it will be your job to name as many things as you can think of that are like what I tell you.' The items were:

1. 'all the round things you can think of'
2. 'all the things you can think of that will make a noise'
3. 'all the square things you can think of'
4. 'all the things you can think of that move on wheels'.

Alternate uses
'In this game, I am going to name an object . . . and it will be your job to tell me lots of different ways that the object would be used.' The items were:

1. newspaper
2. knife
3. automobile tyre—'either the tube or the outer part'
4. a cork
5. shoe
6. button
7. door key
8. key

Similarities
'In this game I am going to name two objects, and I will want you to think of all the ways that these two objects are alike.' The items were:

1. potato and carrot
2. cat and mouse
3. train and tractor
4. milk and meat
5. grocery store and restaurant
6. violin and piano

[1] WISC=Wechsler Intelligence Scale for Children.

7. radio and telephone
8. watch and typewriter
9. curtain and rug
10. desk and table

Pattern meanings
'In this game I am going to show you some drawings. After looking at each one, I want you to tell me all the things you think each complete drawing could be.' There were seven items, one of which is illustrated in Fig. 8:3.

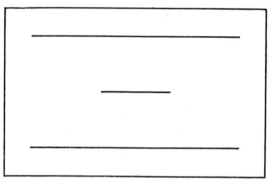

Figure 8:3

A stimulus in the 'pattern meanings' procedure of Wallach and Kogan.

Line meanings
'I am going to show you some lines and after you have looked at each one, I want you to tell me all the things it makes you think of.' There were seven items, one of which is illustrated in Fig. 8:4.

For each child on each measure the total number of responses, and the number of unique responses, were recorded—unique being defined literally as the only response of its kind, to that particular item, among the 151 children.

The creativity measures were found to be substantially inter-correlated, as were the intelligence measures: and these correlations were higher than those between intelligence and creativity. 'We find that the ten creativity indices are very strongly inter-correlated. Indeed, 43 of the 45 correlations in the table are significant beyond the 0·05 level, and 41 of the 45 beyond the 0·01 level.' As for the reliabilities, the creativity measures were found to be reliable by both split-half, and item-sum techniques. The intelligence measures, being from known tests, were known to be reliable.

It may be concluded that Wallach and Kogan have demonstrated the existence of a dimension of creativity, defined in terms of the

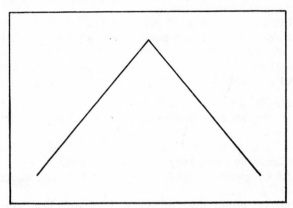

Figure 8:4

A stimulus in the 'line meanings' procedure of Wallach and Kogan.

production of associations, as assessed by total number and unique-ness, and that this dimension is independent of intelligence as conventionally measured. This was found in the sexes considered separately, as well as in the sample as a whole. The results are summarised in Table 8:1.

TABLE 8:1

	Total Sample (N=151)	Boys (N=70)	Girls (N=81)
Correlations among creativity measures	0·41	0·34	0·50
Correlations among intelligence measures	0·51	0·50	0·55
Correlations between creativity and intelligence measures	0·09	0·05	0·13

In the light of these findings, it is possible to distinguish four groups. High Intelligence–High Creativity; High Intelligence–Low Creativity; Low Intelligence–High Creativity; Low Intelligence–Low Creativity. (To be denoted: *HI–HC*; *HI–LC*; *LI–HC*; *LI–LC*).

This was done by converting scores on individual measures to standard scores and summing the results. The distributions were then dichotomised at their medians to yield the four groups to be studied. Numbers were approximately equal in each cell, and the ages did not differ significantly.

The two observers then independently rated the behaviour of the children in school on a 9-point scale, on specified behaviour dimensions e.g., attention-seeking; willingness to contribute to discussion; social confidence; involvement in academic work. The findings for girls, by way of example, were as follows:

The *HI–HC* group are the highest achievers, and most socially confident: they are also the most disruptive, possibly through being most 'alive'.

The *LI–HC* group are least confident and self-assured, least good at academic work. They are also disruptive.

The *LI–LC* group are academically poor, but more assured than the *LI–HC* group.

The *HI–LC* group are confident and assured. They are sought out as friends by others, but do not themselves seek friends. They are not disruptive. Academically they are good.

Other differences were found in the reasons for grouping objects together, whether 'physical-descriptive' or 'thematic' (what you can use them all for). Differences here were observed in boys. The *HI–LC* group avoided thematic classification; all other groups employed thematic classification. Other studies indicated that the *HI–LC* group were *avoiding* thematic classification.

The level of anxiety of the subjects, both as self-reported and as measured, was also obtained. It was found that *HC* groups (independent of intelligence level) were between the *HI–LC* group (low) and *LI–LC* group (high).

Creativity was also found (in boys) to be inversely related to defensiveness about one's negative feelings, and to ability to interpret emotionality in others.

The overall findings may be summarised as follows: the children high on both creativity and intelligence exercised within themselves both control and freedom, showing both maturity and childlike behaviour as appropriate. Those high on creativity but low on intelligence were 'in angry conflict with themselves and with their school environment' and were 'beset by feelings of unworthiness and inadequacy'; however, they could 'blossom forth cognitively' in an atmosphere free from stress. Children low on creativity but high on intelligence were 'addicted' to school achievement to the extent of perceiving school failure as catastrophic. The children low on both creativity and intelligence were 'basically bewildered' and engaged in various defensive manoeuvres, ranging from intense social activity to withdrawal and psychosomatic illness.

A methodological criticism that must be made of this research is that Wallach and Kogan defined creativity in terms of fluency and originality of respones, finding fluency and originality to be related. Now word fluency is usually regarded as one of the primary factors of intelligence, so it is difficult to see how they substantiate the claim that they have measured creativity. It would have been more convincing had they equated the children on this variable before seeking other differential criteria of creativity.

One other point that may give us pause is their isolation of groups displaying high creativity in association with low intelligence. Traditionally creativity has been thought of as a way of using intelligence, and Guilford for one finds it hard to separate from traditional problem-solving. Newell, Shaw and Simon also find no differences in kind between the thinking of creative and non-creative individuals. These considerations may make us wonder if if makes sense to regard creativity as a dimension at all. That is to say, even if we accept the experimental findings of Wallach and Kogan and others as establishing the existence of an intellectual dimension distinct from intelligence as conventionally measured, we may be unjustified in calling this 'creativity'.

If the experimental work described raises doubts, this is even more the case with much of the work done in recent years under the banner of 'creativity research'. The field has attracted the woolly-minded and half-educated as well as the out-and-out charlatan. Unfortunately the creativity lobby has had wide-ranging effects in educational psychology as we shall see.

It would be impossible to summarise all the work that has been done in recent years on creativity (whether the quality of the work justifies lengthy consideration is left for the interested reader to decide for himself) so we shall limit ourselves to a few illustrations. A useful survey of empirical research (including the Wallach and Kogan work) is provided by Freeman, Butcher, and Christie. An attempt to provide a single, critical, integrated review has been made by Taylor (1964a). Taylor has also edited the proceedings of the Utah Creativity Research Conferences (Taylor 1964b; Taylor and Williams). Anderson has performed a similar service for a symposium held at Michigan State University, to which he contributed a paper of his own on creativity in human relationships. The flavour of this paper can be gathered from the knowledge that this form of creativity encompasses the Magna Charta [*sic*], the Bill of Rights, arranging car pools, keeping on good terms with the neighbours, and so on. A similar catholicity of approach is adopted by Barron (1968), whose aim is to treat his subjects' philosphy of life as a psychological attribute. Barron has contributed a paper to the Fifth Utah Conference (Taylor, 1964b) dealing with the liberating effects of laughter induced by injections of psilocybin obtained from the celebrated 'sacred mushroom' (or one of them: *Psilocybe mexicana* Heim, not *Amanita muscaria*). Rugg has a conception of a transliminal mind, the 'creative centre of the conscious-unconscious continuum' which includes light hypnosis but excludes medium and deep trance states. He writes of 'opening the trance vestibules' and deals with Taoism and yoga. Possibly less earnest is De Bono, whose approach to 'lateral thinking' includes the technique of saying 'Po' before factual statements of supposed impossibilities to liberate thought from its conventional prison.[1]

'Creativity' appears to be a modern shiboleth, particularly among American educational psychologists who have been influenced by the views of Kubie. Kubie distinguishes between the conscious, the unconscious (which is the deep-lying source of neurotic anxieties), and the preconscious (a source of creative combinations of ideas). Freud also distinguished between conscious, unconscious and preconscious, but he did not assign this creative role to the preconscious: for Freud, to call an idea preconscious meant that it could easily be called into consciousness, as distinct from unconscious ideas, which could not. Kubie believes that we can increase the creative contribution of the preconscious by freeing the individual of neurotic conflicts.

Kubie's ideas have had the effect of establishing creativity as a criterion of good educational practice.[2] A good illustration of this view can be found in the introduction by Jones to his selection of essays on *Contemporary Educational Psychology*.

One is justified in asking three questions about this movement:

1. is this stress on creativity good for the child;
2. does it contribute materially to the child's educational development;
3. are the children's productions valid creations?

[1] This prison has, we should remember, contained such intellects as those of Galileo, Newton, and Einstein.

[2] Kubie's views may be regarded as the culmination of the movements towards cultural primitivism and anti-intellectualism, which can be traced to the influence of Rousseau, and which have reached their apogee in our own day. For a history of these movements see Boas.

In answer to the first question many people would agree that any technique that helps children to understand their own impulses is good. This view is not universally shared and there are those who argue that it is not good to dwell on one's own inner nature, and that one should adopt what they call a 'commonsense' view of things. The view that self-examination is a bad thing is associated with the rigidity of temperament that results from an authoritarian upbringing. Authoritarianism and discipline were more characteristic of previous ages than of today, and it is important to appreciate the reason for this. Earlier ages believed that strict control of upbringing was necessary in order to avoid moral degradation of the child. In other words they adopted the pessimistic view that human nature left to its own resources would become corrupt.[1]

The view of today is that, if one does not acknowledge one's own impulses for evil as well as good, the impulses will be repressed into the unconscious. Then they will be projected on to other people, so that one will believe others to have the evil nature that one cannot acknowledge in oneself. The result will be hatred and aggression.

This unfortunate result will be avoided if one learns fully to understand and accept oneself, and modern education seeks to help children to do this from the earliest years. Whether the stress on creativity is the best way to do this is a question that we have no firm evidence to answer. It seems to be assumed that it is and that no demonstration is needed. A further question that needs to be answered is whether the present methods of teacher training are the most suitable for preparing teachers for this sort of work, or indeed whether the school is the most suitable environment for this activity. There are no firm answers to these questions, and these questions are topics of current controversy in educational psychology. This controversy illustrates the fact that education inevitably reflects society's views of human nature. Earlier ages believed that man must be constrained if he were not to become corrupt. Today we believe that, whilst self-control is desirable, this control must arise from self-understanding. Education is now seen as having the function of preventing mental illness by promoting mental hygiene.

In attempting to answer the first question ('Is the stress on creativity good for the child?') we have partly answered the second question ('Does it contribute materially to the child's educational development?') It is assumed by modern educators that, if the material to be learnt is linked to the child's spontaneous fantasies, this material will be seen to be more meaningful, and hence more easily learnt. It is certainly true that material will be more easily assimilated if the

[1] See the account of Wolfenstein's views in Chapter 6 of this book. See also Boas.

child is able to relate it to his own experience but there is a limit to the operation of this principle. What applies to the primary school may not apply to the secondary school, where the subjects to be learnt are not of a nature to be linked to spontaneous fantasies. What is true of secondary school education is even truer of university education. Our question may be reformulated to read: 'Does an early stress on creativity help or hinder the development of good learning habits in later life?' To this question one cannot give an answer, because there is no relevant evidence. This is a topic on which research is urgently needed. In passing we may note that it is the experience of the present author that in many schools, the stress on creative fantasy appears to preclude instruction in how to communicate verbally.

To the third question ('Are the children's productions valid creations?') the author is inclined to reply 'No'. This, however, is not a subject to which evidence is relevant, but is a matter of opinion. The author is inclined to feel that the fact that all young children can draw or paint something or other is of no more significance than that they produce fantastic words that are not part of any language. This point of view is opposed to the view that creativity is innate in us all, and that it is destroyed, in most people, by formal education. The only conceivable evidence for this view is that more children create than do adults; but we can only accept this as evidence if we regard children's productions as of the same nature as the productions of creative adults. It is this equation of the productions of children and adults that is challenged here.

It is challenged because adult creativity, at least in the fields of science and scholarship, always involves considerable erudition. E. G. Boring (1950b) includes erudition as one of the attributes of genius. Others that he lists include an interest in novel relations, alertness and the ability to keep one's thinking directed to the point at issue.

To what extent these attributes apply to artistic productions is not clear. Almost certainly an interest in novel relations, and alertness, are found in all creative people. Furthermore the ability to direct one's attention to the essential point of one's work is universal among artists, superficial appearances to the contrary. Biographies of artists all stress that, however disorganised an artist's life may be, he is in deadly earnest with respect to his work. Anyone who has known artists can confirm this from his own experience. Erudition may seem less important, particularly in these days of abstract art and expressionism. However, voices have been raised against this movement (see Snaith).

The subject of creativity in scientists and artists is too large to be discussed in detail but all students of the subject agree with Poincaré's analysis, that it involves two periods of conscious work separated by unconscious work. Wallas later made two divisions of Poincaré's period of unconscious work, and gave us the familiar four steps: preparation, incubation, inspiration, verification. One's impression of the 'creativity work' in schools is that it concentrates on the unconscious work to the neglect of the conscious work (see Ghiselin).

For an artist the 'verification' of his idea is embodied in the work that he produces, which has traditionally been supposed to require technique. Here we come to the crux of an important controversy. There seem at present to be two approaches to art. One type of artist produces works to match his vision, another tries to free his unconscious to produce work, hoping to recognise a valid work of art if and when this is produced.[1] Artists of the second type seem to be dominant at the present time, and it appears to be their view of the nature of artistic activity that inspires the teachers who encourage creative fantasies in young children. The author's opinion is that, even if we can regard productions of the type we are discussing as artistically valid, we are misled by superficial resemblances if we regard the efforts of very young children in this direction as of fundamentally the same nature as adult art.

Thus what appears to some writers to be a straightforward psychological question (is creativity a dimension?) can be shown to be one aspect of a much wider issue involving aesthetic considerations and social policy. If the arguments can be briefly summarised it is by saying that *creativity is a value judgement.* We call an artist or scientist creative not simply because he produces work or ideas that no one has previously produced, but because we believe the productions to have worth. Failure to recognise what is involved in our use of the terms 'creative', 'creativity', 'original', and 'originality' makes nonsense of the claim, adduced by Ray and endorsed by many others, that creativity and originality are not only the hope for the future of man, but can be fostered by psychological and educational techniques.

It may be argued that value judgements have no place in science, but anything produced by human beings for human use must be subject to the criterion of value. If this is true of material goods it must, *a fortiori*, be true of ideas. For psychologists to study that aspect of human intellectuality that is commonly called 'creative' without recognising the value aspect of this judgement results in sterility of research. As an illustration let us examine an experiment discussed favourably by Ray (the experiment is by Mednick). Subjects are

[1] See papers by van Gogh and Ernst in Ghiselin.

asked to give a word association to the stimulus word 'table'. They are asked to do this again and again, giving a different response each time; eventually they give original associations. For example, the first six associations of one subject were: chair, cloth, wood, leg, food, Mabel.

This list should give us pause. The last response 'table-Mabel' is what is commonly known as a 'clang response', which has traditionally been regarded as indicative of low intellectual capacity. In other words, the result of this training for originality was to make a subject produce a response that was low in his response hierarchy for a very good reason, namely that it was of poor quality! Such responses can only be accepted as evidence of original thinking by experimenters who are prepared to employ the concept in an entirely empty sense.

The anthropologists have been accused of stripping the word 'culture' of all significance. Some psychologists have been guilty of the same disservice to the term 'creativity'. It is hoped that this chapter will restore some meaning to this much abused word.

9

CONCEPTUALISING

The study of concepts owes much to philosophy as well as to psychology. The philsosophy in question is that associated with the later work of Wittgenstein, which was concerned, among other topics, with 'language games'. (For a general discussion of Wittgenstein's work see Pitcher.) To understand what is involved in the study of language as a game, let us consider the game of cricket. Cricket is played according to a set of rules agreed by both teams, and these rules define the game. If one fielder starts dribbling the ball and another tackles him, as in soccer, then they are no longer playing cricket. In breaking the rules they have ceased to play the game. In much the same way if I say 'my head hurts' I am abiding by the rules of English grammar: but if I should say 'my hurt heads' I should not only be breaking the rules, I should have ceased to talk English. Of course it is possible to break the rules deliberately for humorous or other effect, as in the celebrated definition of the oboe (attributed to Sam Goldwyn among others) as 'an ill wind that nobody blows good'. The essential point of rule-breaking is that it can be recognised as such. Normal speech is not constrained like physical phenomena, which are said to 'obey' physical laws: instead it conforms to rules. Most human behaviour is rule-conforming in this sense, rather than law-obeying in the physical sense (Toulmin, 1968).

Let us now consider the position of a spectator called from the crowd to join in the game as a replacement for an injured player. We may picture him as an American, ignorant of the game, but too polite to refuse. This obliging individual has to work out for himself the rules of the game, by abstracting certain features of the other players' behaviour, and generalising from them. Suppose that at the end of the game we ask him what is meant by the terms: 'run', 'l.b.w.', 'bye', 'stumped', and so on. Assuming him to be intelligent, we shall find that he has a fair idea of what the terms mean, even though he may not express them in the words of the rule-book.

Now let us move the discussion to a more abstract level and ask if he has 'concepts' of a run, a bye, etc. If he could express the notions with some degree of coherence, it would generally be agreed that he had. However, he may have been able to play reasonably successfully without being able to give a coherent account of what he was doing, and not even be able to identify runs and byes from definitions read to him. Should we in such circumstances allow that he had the appropriate concepts? Most philosophers would say that he had not, as they would wish to make the ability to express ideas verbally part of the definition of 'having concepts'. In this they would be opposed to some psychologists, e.g., Carroll (1964a), who argues that children acquire many concepts before attaining language (although he does put 'concept' in inverted commas).

Let us now consider two other features of this example. In the first place our hypothetical spectator-cum-player may be supposed to understand that he has been playing a game, and that the activity of playing cricket is only part of a wider sphere of activities, which include his having gone to the cricket ground in the first place, going home afterwards and so on. In the second place the position of this individual is analogous to that of every child who finds himself growing up in a world of adults and older children, speaking a language whose rules *they* understand, but which *he* must learn as he goes along. The analogy breaks down here, as all analogies must eventually, as the language game is not encapsulated like that of cricket, but refers at most points to sensory experience, not least in the matter of names. Thus the child hears some things referred to as 'tables' others as 'chairs', and quite different sorts of things as 'dogs' and 'cats'. Eventually he develops a fairly clear idea of what is meant by these things.

At what point can we say that he has concepts of tables, chairs, etc? Most people would probably agree that a child had a concept of 'dog', for instance, when he could point out examples of dogs, clearly indicating that he knew that they were called dogs and that they differed from things that were not dogs. For instance, the author's two-year-old niece once pointed out to him all the dogs that they met on a walk, in the following terms: 'that's a French dog' (a poodle); 'that's a Chinese dog' (a chow); 'that's a Yorkshire dog' (a terrier). Although she would have been quite unable to define 'dog' in abstract terms, she clearly had a concept of what constituted a dog.

   Psychological studies of conceptual thinking may for convenience
be divided into two groups. First we have studies of children's
developing conceptual grasp of the world: these studies are associated
with the work of the Russian psychologists, currently represented by
Luria (sometimes spelt Luriya), and the Swiss epistemologist Jean
Piaget. In the second group we have laboratory investigations, which
mostly fit the following pattern: the investigator sets up a more or
less artificial concept, based on experimental materials, and the
subject has to work out what it is. Studies of this sort are usually
referred to as studies of *concept attainment*. Concept attainment
studies may be further divided into two subgroups: more or less
isolated empirical studies done before 1950; and the studies of
strategies in concept attainment deriving from the mid-50s work of
Bruner, Goodnow, and Austin.

   Let us first briefly examine some studies of concept attainment. So
many experiments have been performed that only two of the pre-
1950 studies will be selected for the purpose of illustration. (More
illustrations will be found in Miller, 1951, ch. 11; Woodworth and
Schlosberg, ch. 20. For a more recent survey and critical discussion
see Bourne.) Suppose that we show children shapes with nonsense
names as in Fig. 9:1. The children are told that *MEF*s and *TOV*s
are *VIC*s; *YOP*s and *ZIL*s are *DAX*es; and that *VIC*s and *DAX*es
are *XIP*s. The problem is to say what features *MEF* and *TOV* have
in common to make them both classifiable as *VIC*; what common
features permit the classification of *YOP* and *ZIL* as *DAX*; and
why *VIC* and *DAX* may both be classified as *XIP*.

   Welch and Long, who conducted this experiment with 45 children
aged from five to seven in 1940, found that all the subjects learnt the
names of the figures, so that they could select a *MEF*, *TOV*, *YOP*
and *ZIL* from a pile on request. All but three could also, if asked for
a *VIC* give either a *MEF* or a *TOV*; and when asked for a *DAX*
give a *YOP* or a *ZIL*. However only 22 of the children, when asked
for a *XIP*, could give any one of *MEF*, *TOV*, *YOP*, or *ZIL*. To do so
would require a grasp of the concept of 'regular figure', which was
too difficult for most of the children.

   An experiment by Heidbreder studied the generalisation of attained
concepts. Children were shown a series of pictures, as in Fig. 9:2.
Each picture was named by the experimenter, the relevant names
being shown in Fig. 9:2. They were then shown another series of
pictures as if they were the first series, and the children were asked
to name them, that is, the test was presented as one of memory. This
series, which we may call the test series, is shown in Fig. 9:3. Children
were found to name the figures as if they had seen them before,

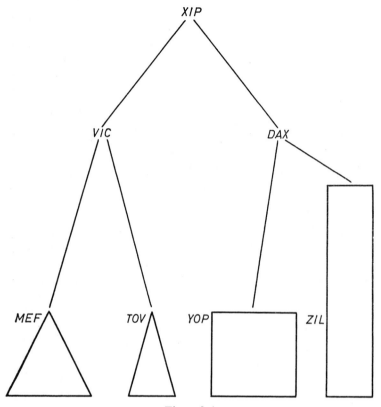

Figure 9:1

Shapes with nonsense names (after Welch and Long).

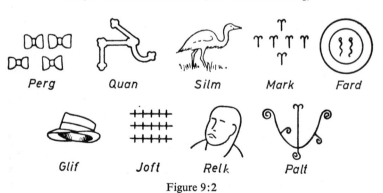

Figure 9:2

Examples of Heidbreder's experimental figures and nonsense names.

indicating that they had abstracted the qualities of '4-ness' from Perg, 'face-ness' from Relk, and so on, and generalised to new situations.

Figure 9:3
Examples of Heidbreder's test series.

Let us now turn to the more recent work of Bruner, Goodnow, and Austin. They define a concept as a category, and distinguish two sorts of category:

1. *Identity classes*, in which a variety of stimuli are classed as the 'same' (e.g., the boy and the grown man are the same person);

2. *Equivalence classes*, in which different items are treated as equivalent for some purpose or another (for instance, lettuces, tomatoes and turnips, are all vegetables).

We classify objects as identical or equivalent by discriminating certain attributes and using them as the basis of classification. We learn new concepts by identifying in an object those attributes that the object must have in order to belong to one category rather than another; having identified these attributes one can recognise other objects as belonging to that category, or not belonging, as the case may be.

Attributes vary in kind. Some are sensory: an orange, for example, has the attribute of colour within a certain range of yellowish reds. Others are abstract: 'speeding' means going at faster than an agreed speed in a built-up area. Concepts vary both in their kind of defining attributes, and in the ways in which those attributes are combined in the definition. Concepts may be *conjunctive* (e.g., 'X is anything with properties a *and* b', etc.); *disjunctive* (e.g., 'Y is anything with *either* property a *or* property b', etc.); or *relational*. To form a relational concept the subject must combine two or more attributes. In the Semeonoff–Vigotsky test, for instance, the subject is asked to sort a number of blocks, differing in shape, colour, height, and cross-section, into four piles. Solution of the problem requires the subject to realise that the principle of grouping in *bulk*, i.e., height times cross-section. Relational concepts pose particular difficulties for brain-damaged patients (see Chapter 11). In what follows we shall illustrate the experimental work mainly with reference to conjunctive concepts.

In the experiments the material comprises cards bearing one of the shapes shown in Fig. 9:4. There may be up to three, i.e., a card may have one cross, two crosses, or three crosses: or else one circle, two circles, or three circles; or one square, two squares, or three squares. They may be in one of three colours (black, red, or green), and have borders consisting of one, two, or three lines. Thus there are

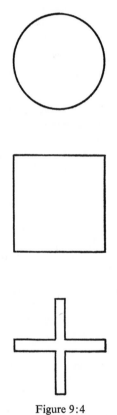

Figure 9:4

Shapes used in the concept attainment studies of Bruner, Goodnow, and Austin.

3 (shapes) × 3 (number of shapes) × 3 (colours) × 3 (borders) = 81 different cards. The experimenter selects from these possibilities a concept such as 'a card with two squares and a double border', and shows the subject cards in random order, each time telling the subject whether or not this particular card exemplifies the concept. Thus in the example given, any card with two squares and a double border, irrespective of colour, would exemplify the concept: but any card without two squares, or with two squares but a single or triple border, would not. From such information the subject must deduce the concept.

To do this the subject employs certain strategies to solve the problem with the optimum conditions of minimising time, effort, errors, and uncertainties. The subject may not have worked out that this is what he is doing, but it is fair to characterise his activity in this way. We argue that, if he is to achieve these objectives, he must adopt certain *ideal strategies*; the strategies that he does in fact adopt, may depart from these ideal strategies in ways that we can investigate.

The ideal strategies are of two sorts: 1. *Focussing*, or wholist; 2. *Scanning*, or partist. With the focussing strategy the subject takes the first instance that the experimenter informs him exemplifies the concept, and declares that this is the whole concept. For instance a subject is shown a card with two red squares and a double border. The subject declares that the hypothesis is 'two red squares and a double border'. If the concept is simply 'two squares and a double border' the experimenter will inform the subject that he is wrong. The experimenter shows the subject a card with two green squares and a double border, informing him that this is an example of the concept. The subject now knows that colour is irrelevant, and correctly declares that the concept is 'two squares and a double border'.

In practice the subject will probably not declare his hypothesis until after a number of exemplifying and non-exemplifying instances have been shown to him. Nevertheless he will proceed to guess in the manner described. The simplicity of this strategy lies in the fact that an instance that he is told does not exemplify the concept can be ignored, as the subject proceeds by eliminating from successive exemplifying instances all features that are shown to be superfluous in his original hypothesis.

The scanning strategy involves more mental effort. Essentially the subject selects one feature of the first card that he is told exemplifies the concept, and makes that the basis of his hypothesis. Then he expands his hypothesis when faced with instances that contradict it. To continue the example already given, if he is first shown a card with two black squares and a double border he guesses that the concept is 'squares'. He is shown a card with three squares, and told that this does not exemplify the concept; clearly, then, 'squares' is a wrong hypothesis. The subject must now formulate a hypothesis consistent with all that has gone before, for example 'two squares'. He is then shown a card with two squares and triple border and told that this is not an exemplar. He then forms a new hypothesis. In this way, he will eventually arrive at the solution.

The experimental technique that we have described is called the *reception* technique, because the subject receives information in the order chosen by the experimenter. An alternative way is the *selection* technique, in which the subject picks up the cards in the order that *he*, not the experimenter, decides, and demands to know whether or not the card that he has selected exemplifies the concept. Either technique may, of course, be employed with conjunctive or disjunctive concepts. Another variation, employing the reception technique, is not to provide sufficient information to permit the subject to formulate a hypothesis with certainty; in this way one can study the ways in which subjects use information as the basis of probable judgements.

The results of experiments such as those that we have described show that about two-thirds of subjects adopt the focussing strategy, but that, whichever method they adopt, they tend to be consistent in following through the strategy to the solution, at least as far as conjunctive concepts are concerned. Disjunctive concepts prove more difficult, because the search for common elements is inappropriate when the concept is such as: '*either* two squares with a double border *or* three squares with a triple border'. Bruner believes that disjunctive concepts are particularly difficult to attain in a culture that looks for common causes of common effects, because the correct hypothesis about a disjunctive concept is correct for more than one reason.

We have described the work of Bruner and his colleagues at some length, as it is the foundation of the contemporary psychological investigation of concept attainment. More recent work is to a large extent an extension of these original investigations, and includes the formulation of mathematical models for predicting the behaviour of subjects in situations involving probable judgements. We shall not describe these studies, as our object is not to present an exhaustive survey of the material, but to illustrate the main directions of the work done in this field. The reader who wishes to learn more details will find them discussed by Bourne; Duncan also has a section on this topic.

Let us now turn to studies of intellectual development that are relevant to the theme of conceptual thinking. As we have mentioned already there are two major schools: the Russian and the Genevan. Both are of long standing, as the Russian school was founded in the 1920s (at the time when Piaget was beginning his investigations) by Vigotsky, although the work is best known today through the writings of his pupil Luria. A third school, headed by Professor Bruner of Harvard (whose studies of concept attainment in adults we have just examined), is of more recent date, and may be viewed as a counterbalance to the excesses of the other two. The essential difference between the schools lies in the emphasis that they place on the role of language in intellectual development: the Russians regard language as virtually a *sine qua non* of mental growth; the Genevans under Piaget often talk as if they believe that the intellect would develop in its accustomed fashion even in the absence of language; whereas the Harvard school regards language as a valuable tool employed by the individual in shaping his experience (for a brief account of the Harvard viewpoint see Bruner, 1964; a longer account is given by Bruner *et al.*, 1966; for a brief general discussion see Boyle, 1969, ch. 9). Inasmuch as Piaget's work is primarily an attempt to construct a philosophy of knowledge, based upon psychological observations, and only secondarily a contribution to psychology as such, we shall treat it separately (in the next chapter). We shall conclude this chapter by describing the Russian work (based on Luria, 1961) which Toulmin (1968) regards as particularly relevant to the philosophical analysis of conceptual thinking that we described at the beginning of this chapter.

Luria believes that the aim of psychology should be the study of the formation of mental processes. This development is not inevitable (a view opposed to that of Piaget). Mental activities are conditioned from the outset by social relationships: social contacts, largely through speech, give the child new ways of organizing his mental activities. The earliest social groups comprise two individuals (mother and child), but the mental functioning developed in the two-person group gradually becomes extended to form the essence of human mental activity.

Luria regards language as of very great importance in mental development (indeed, this is the major characteristic of the Russian school). By the use of spoken language the child can modify his perceived environment to facilitate interaction with it. In one experiment to illustrate this, children were shown pictures of aeroplanes on grey or yellow backgrounds; they were told to press a rubber bulb when the background was yellow but not when it was grey. This task is normally very difficult or impossible for children under 5 years of age, as they are distracted by the main feature (the plane) and ignore the background. However, if they are instructed in terms such as the following: 'when it's yellow the sun's shining, so we press to make the plane fly; when it's grey it's raining, and the plane can't take off, so we don't press' even some 3-year-olds successfully make the discrimination. In another experiment, children of 12 to 30 months were asked to discriminate between red and green boxes; they were unable to do this consistently until they were taught the names of the colours.

As the child grows older he no longer needs to speak in order to solve such problems. Electromyographic records show that the rudiments of speech are still present (see the references to the work of Jacobson and of Max) and, in the face of difficulties, adults as well as children will 'think out loud'. Normally, however, speech becomes internalised at around the 7th year, and Luria regards the internalisation of speech as characteristic of the development of most of the higher forms of intellectual performance. Interaction with adults can facilitate speech internalisation at an earlier age than normal; in this way, mental development can be encouraged. This finding is important in the light of the Russian view on the assessment of intellectual performance, namely that a child's capacity should be judged in terms of how far he can make use of adult help in solving problems, and the extent to which he can apply the results of such help to other situations.

Pavlov spoke of language as a 'second signalling system', by which he meant that animals respond directly to signals from the environment, whereas human beings use language to abstract and generalise environmental signals, and then respond to these generalisations. Thus language facilitates the development of conditioned responses, because the response becomes incorporated into an appropriate verbal system. This view, which is generally accepted by Russian psychologists, is radically different from the approach of Skinner and his followers (see Chapter 2), who attempt to explain the development of the verbal systems themselves in terms of the laws of conditioning. The Russian view does not *explain* language, but resembles Chomsky's approach in accepting language as a fact of (human) nature, in terms of which other facts can be explained.

Whatever the truth of the matter as far as the origin of language is concerned, it is undeniable that language does often stand between us and our reactions to the environment. Not only does it pick out certain features to which we respond, it may help us to inhibit some actions and regulate others. Little girls will often be observed talking to their dolls in such terms as the following: 'You must not do that if Mummy says it's naughty', thus simultaneously demonstrating the ability to classify an action as 'prohibited' and reinforcing the use of language for this purpose. One will also hear 'You may only have a sweet if you finish your greens', which represents a more complex level of understanding, namely that of conditionals. (These two illustrations are the author's.) Luria describes a number of experiments in which children of 3 years or under were required to press rubber bulbs in response to one stimulus but not another. The tasks proved very difficult until the experimenters helped the children to analyse the situations verbally. The ability to use language in the analysis of a situation appears at about 5 years of age, but language can be used much earlier in what Luria calls an 'impellant' fashion; the child is asked to say 'go' every time he presses the bulb, so if he is required to press twice he is instructed to say 'go, go'. Using spoken language in an impellant way under adult guidance enables children of under 5 years to follow complicated instructions (e.g., 'when the light flashes, press twice') which would otherwise prove impossible to master. (For a discussion of Luria's more recent work on brain functions see Chapter 11.)

In this chapter we have examined the strategies that adults employ in solving conceptual tasks, and the process by which children use their language to make sense of their environment. This process must precede the ability to talk coherently about that environment, which is the criterion that one employs when deciding that a normal individual, without language loss from brain damage or other cause, has concepts of significant features of his environment. In terms of the discussion with which we opened this chapter, Luria's work offers one interpretation of how children learn language games and their place in behaviour games generally. Piaget's work, to which we now turn, offers another.

GENETIC EPISTEMOLOGY

Epistemology is the study of knowledge from a philosophical point of view; it concerns such questions as 'of what does knowing consist?' and 'what can we be truly said to *know* rather than to act upon as if we knew?' and so on. Genetic epistemology, associated with the name of Jean Piaget, is an attempt to shed light on these questions by a study of the developing intellect: the term 'genetic' in this context refers to the development of intellectual structures from their beginnings into their mature form.

A study of intellectual structures may seem a little strange to psychologists who are used to thinking in terms of mental functions, and for many years Piaget's work was regarded politely but not too seriously. In the past twenty years, however, the climate of opinion has changed, partly because of an increasing realisation that human beings are biological systems, which have structural laws and are modifiable only within limits. This view is a reaction to the opinion widely held in the 1920s and 30s that man is infinitely malleable by education and experience. That opinion is still held by Russian thinkers, and thus Piaget's view is opposed to the views of Luria and his colleagues. It appears to many who are not committed to either school that both exaggerate their positions: almost certainly man is not as malleable as some extreme environmentalists suggest, nor is he as unmodifiable as Piaget often seems to imply.

The difficulty in interpreting Piaget's view is that the questions mentioned in the first paragraph sometimes seem relevant and sometimes do not. Essentially Piaget is constructing a philosophy of mind, but he often talks as if his system is a *psychology* of mind. If it is psychology, empirical issues are highly relevant: if it is a philosophy then, although empirical objections are not irrelevant, they do not have the same force. As a result of this ambiguity, Piaget's system of thinking is very difficult to criticise.

When Piaget first took an interest in psychology in order to answer epistemological questions he intended to devote about five years to the study. In fact he spent about forty years investigating the development in children of concepts of space, time, number, and so on. It would be impossible in a short space to give a full account of this lifetime's work, and the reader interested in details is referred to Flavell. Here we shall outline the main features of the developmental studies, before turning to a discussion of Piaget's latest summary statement of his views.

Piaget believes that the intellect is organised. This would follow from the fact that the intellect is part of animate nature, and animate nature is characterised by organisation. As far as the intellect is concerned, the organisation has two aspects: organisation of actions with respect to the environment, and organisation of images whereby the individual deals with the environment symbolically. Organisation of actions Piaget calls *schemes*: he calls organisation of images *schemata*. Because the intellect is organised it is adapted to the environment, but the adaptation cannot be static in the face of growth, with its changing demands. The adaptation is modified in two ways: *assimilation*, whereby the schemes and schemata encompass new features of the environment (for instance, if a child can pick up a doll it can pick up a bottle by using the same scheme of actions); and *accommodation*, whereby the schemes and schemata are changed in order to cope with new situations (for example, a child may be able to pick up something within reach, but the first time a toy is placed out of reach, the child must crawl to reach it before picking it up).

The first two years of a child's life are devoted to coming to terms with the physical environment. Piaget calls this the *sensorimotor* phase. As the child interacts with the environment he notices constant features of this interaction: for instance, in counting a pile of pebbles he observes that the number remains the same however he lays them out, whether in a circle or a straight line, and whether he is putting them down or picking them up. He abstracts this information from the situation. In doing so he modifies his intellectual schemata, so that, when he encounters new situations involving physical constants he has a new element upon which to build his view of the world. Piaget calls this process *reflective abstraction*.

Reflective abstraction is a potentially infinite process. In abstracting features of his actions with respect to the world, the child internalises these features. An internalised action Piaget calls an *operation*.

Reflective abstraction can act upon operations, thus creating higher order operations. Piaget sees this as the method whereby the highest intellectual structures develop in an unbroken sequence from the simplest actions of the baby. Naturally this takes a very long time, and the child has to learn to cope with concrete features of the world before he can deal in higher order abstractions: thus *concrete operations* precede *formal operations*. Moreover not everyone develops to the same degree, because just as some people never reach the stage of formal operations, only a few can operate upon formal operations in such a way as to produce a mathematical theorem, which is the form of intellectual structure that seems to interest Piaget particularly (see Beth and Piaget). Nevertheless the process is qualitatively the same in all men: only the quantitative aspects differ.

This view of the development of intellectuality has as an important consequence the fact that one man may be taken as a representative of mankind in general, which may be why Piaget spurns the common practice of employing large numbers of subjects and computing statistics from them. It also means that, if one individual does not illustrate Piaget's view sufficiently clearly, he may be regarded as an unfortunate choice of subject, and ignored in favour of someone who illustrates the view more satisfactorily. This is convenient for Piaget, but causes dissatisfaction among those of his readers who have a more orthodox view of scientific method.

It is convenient to illustrate the consequences of this approach indirectly, by considering the progress of mathematics. Suppose that a mathematician produces a new mathematical entity, which no one has thought of before. We call his work an invention. Let us suppose further that a second mathematician produces a similar mathematical invention, which is of such a nature that the first mathematician's intellectual creation is now seen to follow obviously from the corpus of previous mathematical knowledge. What has appeared to be an *invention* now seems to be a *discovery*. The second mathematician's intellectual creation may suffer a similar change in status as a result of the work of a third mathematician. The progress of mathematics generally is like this. Thus the status of a piece of knowledge is different according to whether one views it from the viewpoint of the individual who first brought it to the attention of others, or from the viewpoint of someone looking at the general corpus of knowledge to see how it all fits together. Some epistemologists have posed the question: 'does the progress of knowledge consist of a succession of inventions or a series of discoveries?' Piaget's approach offers an answer to this question by offering a third possibility, namely that knowledge progresses by a series of intellectual *constructions*: inasmuch as these constructions are developed by reflective abstraction, then so long as they conform to the rules whereby such abstractions are made (for instance, the mathematician must understand the laws of mathematics before he can perform reflective abstractions upon them) the constructions will find a logical place in the corpus of knowledge. In some respects, then, the individual mathematician is of less interest than mathematicians in general; or speaking more generally, the *epistemic subject*, i.e., that which all individuals have in common at a given stage of intellectual development, is more important than any given individual.

We have spoken of inventions and discoveries in the history of mathematics, but the same process is observable in the development of individuals. A child of 5 years who is shown two beakers of equal size filled with liquid to the same level will agree that the amount of liquid is the same in each. If the contents of one are poured into a shallow dish, the child will say that the amounts are no longer the same. At 7 years he will insist that they are the same. Has he discovered this fact? From an adult point of view he has, but from the child's point of view this change in approach represents the invention of a new strategy. The strategy is to ignore appearances in the solution of problems involving physical variables. The child may not, of course, formulate his approach in these terms, but, inasmuch as he is not permitted to measure the quantities, he cannot be said to have *discovered* the solution. A little later, however, the child realises that physical actions are reversible, at least in imagination. In terms of reversibility it is now obvious that the amount of liquid must stay the same, because it can be poured back into the beaker where it will reach the same level as before.

What has happened is that a new intellectual structure has developed, the essential feature of which is the understanding of reversibility. In terms of this new structure, what was previously a puzzle is now obvious. Intellectual development consists of the progressive development of structures, through reflective abstraction: with each development there is a change in status akin to the change of status from invention to discovery. Another way of putting this is in terms of relative formalisation. To employ an analogy with mathematics once more, Euclidean geometry formalised much of the mathematics that had gone before by incorporating it into an abstract system: contemporary mathematics has formalised Euclidean geometry by incorporating it into a system of much greater abstraction. Similarly, in the individual there is a progressive formalisation of intellectual structures.

The illustration of the individual in terms of mathematics generally and vice versa is not incidental but crucial to an understanding of Piaget, who sees the development of the individual as reflecting the development of intellectuality in mankind generally. This provides Piaget with an even stronger justification for regarding individual aberrations as irrelevant to his overall conceptual framework. It also means that Piaget must express this framework in terms that most closely approach certainty and perfection. The terms that he has chosen are those of symbolic logic. It may seem that, if symbolic logic is the chosen framework for explaining intellectual development, psychological observations are irrelevant, but this is not so. Logic is itself a product of intellectual development, and thus must itself be an object of study. This double attitude to logic is not least among the features of Piaget's philosophy that cause difficulty in understanding it.

The system that we have outlined has been developed over many years. It would be wrong to suppose that Piaget is interested only in logical and mathematical thinking, although this appears to be the sort of thinking that interests him most. Unfortunately the most thorough development of Piaget's views, showing their application to biology, sociology, and psychology remains the untranslated *Introduction à l'Épistémologie Génétique* (for a brief account of this large work see Boyle, 1969, ch. 7). The shorter accounts by Piaget concentrate on logic and mathematics. The shortest is a journal article (Piaget, 1961), the most condensed comprises a series of lectures (the Woodbridge lectures) delivered at Columbia University in 1968 (Piaget, 1970). It is on this last account that the rest of this chapter is largely based.

Piaget argues that his genetic epistemology, with its emphasis on development, has advantages over the traditional view of epistemology as the study of knowledge, because scientific knowledge is itself constantly developing. These scientific ideas depend upon fundamental operations, and so psychological knowledge is relevant to understanding scientific progress. As an illustration of the relationship between scientific ideas and fundamental operations we may consider Cantor's development of the theory of infinite numbers. In essence Cantor's contribution to mathematics developed from the realisation that it was possible to place in correspondence sets of numbers such as 'every whole number' and 'every even number' as follows:

(a)	1	2	3	4	5
(b)	2	4	6	8	10

Both (a) and (b) are infinite series. Since they are in one-to-one correspondence they have the same number of objects in them. Yet how is it that the sum of 'all whole numbers' is the same as the sum of 'all even numbers', and what is this sum? Clearly the conventional terminology cannot express it, so Cantor introduced a new term, viz., *aleph-null*. This development was the basis of a new departure in mathematics, yet it was based on the notion of one-to-one correspondence, which is within the grasp of a young child. (For further discussion of Cantor see Kline, ch. 25.)

Piaget argues further that some disputes must be referred to psychological data for their resolution. As an example we may consider the origin of language. The logical positivists (see the discussion of Ayer in Chapter 12 of this book) believed that logic was an extension of language, whereas Chomsky (Chapter 4 *passim*) argues that language is an extension of reason and is, moreover, innate. Piaget's findings have shown that human actions are co-ordinated in such a way that we are justified in describing them as having a logical structure. This structure does not depend upon language, and so Piaget condemns the linguistic philosophers for seeking the origin of logic in language rather than in the co-ordination of actions. He criticises Chomsky for arguing that language is innate, when it would seem more parsimonious to regard it as the outcome of activity. Many disputes have arisen, in Piaget's view, because people have relied upon speculation rather than observation. Clearly it would be an advantage if we could study the development of human thinking from Neanderthal times to the present day but, as such phylogenetic studies are impossible, we must rest content with observations of the ontogenesis of thinking in children.

Confirmation of Piaget's view that behaviour is logically ordered is provided by the group of Paris mathematicians, calling themselves by the collective name of *Bourbaki*, who have been particularly concerned with a study of the foundations of mathematics. In his studies of thinking Piaget discovered organisations that we may call 'groups' and 'groupings'. A group is a set of elements having the following properties. First, however we combine the elements we obtain a member of the set (e.g., considering the set of whole numbers including zero, however we combine them we obtain a whole number); second, the order in which we combine the elements does not affect the result (e.g., $2+3=3+2$); third, one element of the set must be such that, when combined with the others, it leaves their sum unchanged (e.g., adding zero to any combination of integers does not change the sum); and finally, operations on the elements are reversible, there being two sorts of reversibility, viz., *negation* (e.g., $(5+3)-(5+3)=0$) and *reciprocity* (e.g., if $5+3=8$, then $8=5+3$). The thinking of adolescents (from about 11 years) clearly displays an understanding of the properties of groups. The thinking of children aged 6 or 7 does not reach this level of sophistication; for instance, the notion of class inclusion is missing. This can be demonstrated if we show a child 20 wooden beads of which 15 are blue, the rest white; the child can tell us that there are more blue beads than white beads, but is confused by the question 'are there more blue beads than wooden beads?' because he does not see that: wooden beads = blue beads + white beads. Since, however, his thinking is nonetheless organised, albeit imperfectly, we describe his thinking as made up of groupings.

Although the notions of group and groupings are mathematical, Piaget discovered the grouping structure in children independently of the mathematicians. Only after his discovery did he become aware that the Bourbaki mathematicians had isolated what they called 'mother structures', i.e., basic mathematical structures from which all others could be generated. In addition to mother structures dealing with algebraic classes and numbers (corresponding to Piaget's findings of groupings), and with order (corresponding to Piaget's later studies of propositional thinking in adolescents), they include topological structure, dealing with neighbourhoods, boundaries, and so on. These mother structures are of a high degree of abstraction, yet they are the logical foundations of mathematics, from which the corpus of mathematical knowledge may be derived by implication. We know that topological geometry developed late in the history of mathematics, but the notion of such a geometry is logically primitive. As a striking parallel Piaget discovered that children aged 4 years or less understood the principles of topology before they mastered Euclidean geometry: that is to say, they were unable to copy a square, circle, or triangle, but could draw figures indicating that they understood positions and enclosures (see Fig. 10:1).

Piaget makes the claim that the three mother structures (algebraic, order, topological) have natural roots in the thinking of individuals. This is the sort of claim that causes some people to be sceptical of Piaget, because it seems to confuse a *logical* sequence (from mother structures to the corpus of mathematical knowledge) with an *empirical* sequence. We know that, historically speaking, mother structures came after the corpus of mathematical knowledge had been established, and it is not easy to see how the parallels that Piaget adduces permit him to claim ontological priority for such abstractions. However, this topic is one which can be competently discussed only by a mathematician, which the present author is not.

We are on somewhat less controversial ground when we consider Piaget's views on the development of number. The basis of the notion of number is one-to-one correspondence, for instance, if I am counting objects I add the digit 1 every time I encounter an object. There is, however, a difficulty. Suppose I have three apples and two oranges. I can perform the operation $3+2=5$ only by ignoring the

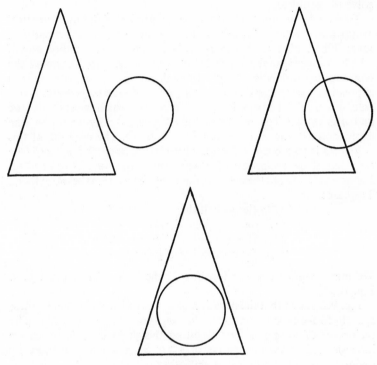

Figure 10:1

Piaget's test figures to show understanding of position and enclosure.

qualitative differences between apples and oranges, but how can I ignore qualitative differences without having the notion of number in the first place? (I have 5, but 5 what?) Piaget's studies have shown that the notion of number depends upon two operations: class inclusion (the idea that 'these belong together') and ordering. Class inclusion and order are thus simpler notions than that of number, which is a synthesis of these simpler notions.

Let us now consider a problem that adolescents can solve, but young children cannot, and see how Piaget's account of the structure of human intellect explains the development. The problem concerns a snail moving forward on a board that is simultaneously moved backwards. If the speeds are matched, the snail will be stationary with respect to the environment. Children presented with this problem and asked to predict the motion of the snail with respect to the board and the environment are confused, but adolescents readily solve the problem.

To see why we must return to the properties of the mathematical group that we listed earlier, and in particular to the property of reversibility. We said that there are two sorts of reversibility, one of which is negation, the other being reciprocity. Let us employ the conventional symbols p and q to illustrate the argument. The expression $p \supset q$ means 'if p then q', or writing it more fully 'if p is true, q is true'. The negation of $p \supset q$ is $p \cdot \bar{q}$, which means 'p is true and q is false'.[1] The reciprocal of $p \supset q$ is $q \supset p$ by definition (the expression $q \supset p$ means 'if q is true, p is true'). The negation of this is $q \cdot \bar{p}$ ('q is true but p is false'). There is a special term for $q \cdot \bar{p}$ (the negation of the reciprocal of $p \supset q$) namely the *correlative* of $p \supset q$. Let us now write out these expressions and the relations between them. They are:

$$p \supset q \text{ (let us call this expression } I\text{)}$$
$$p \cdot \bar{q} \text{ (the negation of } p \supset q, \text{ or } N\text{)}$$
$$q \supset p \text{ (the reciprocal of } p \supset q, \text{ or } R\text{)}$$
$$q \cdot \bar{p} \text{ (the correlative of } p \supset q, \text{ or } C\text{)}$$

We may set out these relationships in the form of a diagram as in Fig. 10:2

Fig. 9:2 shows that the negation of $p \supset q$ is $p \cdot \bar{q}$. Inasmuch as these are all two-way relationships, the negation of $p \cdot \bar{q}$ is $p \supset q$. The reciprocal of $p \supset q$ is $q \supset p$. Negating this gives us $q \cdot \bar{p}$, which we have defined as the correlative of $p \supset q$. So much we have already defined, but the Figure brings out other relationships, e.g., that the reciprocal of $q \supset p$ is $p \supset q$, and that the correlative of $q \supset p$ is $p \cdot \bar{q}$. The relationships between I, N, R, and C constitute a group of transformations, which Piaget calls the 'four group'. According to Piaget the adolescent's thinking must possess this structure before he can solve the problem of the snail on the board. With the structure the solution is easy because we may represent the movement of the snail forward by I; the movement of the board backwards by R;

---

[1] $p \supset q$.   Implication. 'If p is true then q is true'.
$p \cdot q$.   Conjunction. 'Both p and q are true'.
$\bar{p}$.   Negation of p. 'p is false'.
$\bar{q}$.   Negation of q. 'q is false'.

the movement of the snail backwards by N; and the movement of the board forward by C. In these terms, says Piaget, $I R = N C$; in other words the adolescent sees how to combine the four movements so that one compensates for the other.

The reader may wonder if this account of the development of thinking is not too recondite to be very satisfactory. To this there is no answer, because Piaget is not dealing with observables: no one

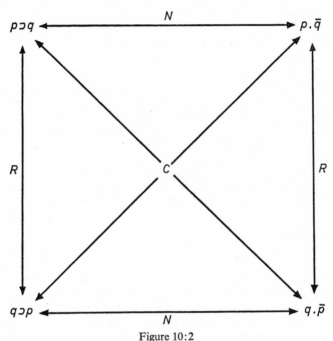

Figure 10:2
The group of transformations, or 4-group.

can obtain direct evidence for the existence of mathematical groups in thinking. Instead Piaget is proposing a model, in terms of which child development can be discussed (Piaget and Inhelder, 1969). The usefulness of a model is not something on which any one person can pronounce, but must stand the test of time. If the generality of thinkers find it useful it will be adopted: if not it will be consigned to the overcrowded limbo of worn-out psychological notions. It is too soon to predict the fate of Piaget's psychology.

Whether or not the model of intellectual development proposed by Piaget is widely adopted one may still find Piaget's empirical observations useful. The observations on space, causality, and other physical variables are well known, and would take too long to summarise here (selected readings are given by Brearley and Hitchfield, and a summary has been made by Beard; Flavell gives the fullest account). Less well known are the observations on the concepts of identity and of speed and time, and these do call for discussion.

The first step in recognising that an object has an identity is the realisation that it continues to exist when it is out of sight. We can say that a child realises this when it searches for an object that is hidden by being placed behind a screen, a form of activity that appears at about seven months. A more advanced step is recognising that an amount of liquid remains the same when this liquid is poured from a beaker to a dish, i.e., appreciation of conservation. The fact that children at first deny that the amounts in the two vessels are identical has led some people to suppose that the children simply do not know how to express themselves, but this is not so. Piaget and his colleagues have shown that training in the use of language does not improve the children's performance (see Bruner, 1964, and the reply by Inhelder *et al.*). Only when the appropriate logical structures have developed does language aid the child.

empiricism

We have seen that Piaget believes that logical structures develop from actions. This is especially clear in the case of the development of the notion of identity. At first a child will regard objects as identical if he can do certain things to them, e.g., a wire is considered to be the same if bent or straight because the child can bend or straighten it. Later he separates the form of an object from his actions with regard to it, and takes change of form as the criterion of change of identity: later still he develops the notion of an object as an abstract entity. This can be shown if we use an instrument known as a stroboscope, which enables one to show a series of rapid alternations of a square and a circle in neighbouring positions. An adult will report seeing an object changing position, whereas a child will say 'It's a circle until it gets almost over to here, and then it becomes a square'. This response indicates that the child has not yet developed a fully logical grasp of the situation; Piaget describes his thinking as exhibiting a 'semi-logic'.

Another ingenious experiment showed that children have two distinct notions of identity: physical and psychological. There are some chemicals that, when placed in water, 'grow' into a plant-like form. If children are asked to draw this form at different stages of its growth, and are then asked if it is the same 'plant', they will deny this. If the same children are asked to make drawings of themselves as they were at different ages, and are asked if the drawings are of the same person, they will agree. The chemical plant was not regarded as having a physical identity continuous throughout its period of growth, whereas the children recognised their own psychological identity.

Finally we come to the notions of speed and time. Speed has traditionally been defined in terms of space covered per unit of time, but as time can only be defined in terms of constant speed, we have a vicious circle. Genetic epistemology shows the way out of this circle by demonstrating that the notion of *movement* at a given speed is intellectually more primitive than either the notion of time or that of speed in the abstract. Young children base their ideas of the speed of movement on the possibility of one object passing another. If one object does not pass another it is not thought to go faster. Piaget arranges for two dolls to go along parallel tracks over each of which is a tunnel. One tunnel is longer than the other, but the apparatus is so arranged that the dolls enter and leave the tunnels together. Five-year-olds insist that the dolls are travelling at the same speed. The tunnels are removed and the experiment repeated, employing the same speeds as before, so that the children can see that one doll passes the other, and they agree that this is going faster. When the tunnels are replaced, the children revert to their previous judgement, viz., that the dolls are moving at the same speed.

The essential feature of the child's view of speed is that it is based upon *ordinal* rather than *metrical* relationships, i.e., the object that moves in front is going faster. Contemporary physics has attempted a new axiomatisation based upon ordinal relationships, which overcomes some of the difficulties with regard to time and speed mentioned earlier. Once more we see a parallel between the most sophisticated developments of science and the study of the thinking of young children.

If the concept of speed develops in children from the more primitive notion of movement, and may be regarded as in intellectual construction, this is also true of the notion of time. The concept of time involves a relationship between something that is done and the speed with which it is done. Young children have no clear understanding of this relationship. For instance, if two dolls are made to hop along a table, starting and stopping at the same time, the children will agree that the time taken is the same for each doll provided that the hops are of equal length. If one doll makes longer hops than the other, the young child will insist that the doll making shorter hops stopped sooner. Older children will say that the dolls started and stopped at the same time, but that the one making the longer hops moved for a longer time (because it moved further). The reasoning seems to be that getting more done involves spending more time.

The development of the abstract concept of time appears after simpler notions have developed and become synthesised. These simpler notions are: first, seriation (*B* comes after *A*, *C* comes after *B*, etc.); second, a form of class inclusion (if *B* follows *A*, and *C* follows *B*, then the interval *AC* must be longer than the interval *AB*). Just as the concept of number is a result of the synthesis of class inclusion and ordering of objects, so the adult concept of time results from the synthesis of seriation and class inclusion of ordinal relationships.

In this highly condensed summary of Piaget's thinking we have discussed a number of illustrations of Piaget's fundamental thesis with regard to concept formation. To reiterate, it is that all concepts arise in the last analysis from the co-ordination of actions. This co-ordination, when represented on the abstract mental plane, constitutes the individual's conceptual view of the world. Language may be used to give an account of this view to others, but conceptual development does not depend upon language, nor can language in any way facilitate it.

THE ROLE OF THE BRAIN
IN LANGUAGE AND THINKING

Life begins when a fertilised egg cell, or ovum, begins repeatedly to divide and subdivide. This process results in a mass of daughter cells, differentiated into three layers, from the outermost of which develop the skin, the sense organs, and the central nervous system, which comprises the brain and spinal cord. (The middle cell layer gives rise to the skeleton and the muscles; whilst the innermost layer is the origin of the vital organs.)

The first stage of the development of the central nervous system (or CNS as it is customarily abbreviated) is the shape of a tube, at the front end of which are three swellings, or vesicles. The front vesicle eventually develops into the *forebrain*, or *prosencephalon*; the middle vesicle becomes the *midbrain* or *mesencephalon*; the last vesicle becomes the *hindbrain* or *rhombencephalon*. The prosencephalon becomes further differentiated into the *diencephalon* and *telencephalon*: the rhombencephalon also differentiates into the *myelencephalon* and the *metencephalon*. From lowest to highest the sequence in the fully developed brain is myelencephalon, metencephalon, mesencephalon, diencephalon, telencephalon.

The metencephalon bears a tripartite structure known as the *cerebellum*, which is important in the control of movement. Apart from the cerebellum we may think of the myelencephalon, metencephalon, mesencephalon and diencephalon as comprising the *brain stem*. The remaining part (the telencephalon) is of particular interest, as it includes the *cerebrum* with its covering layer, the *cerebral cortex*.

The cerebrum comprises two hemispheres each of which controls the opposite side of the body, i.e., the left hemisphere controls the right side and vice versa. The left hemisphere is usually dominant, so most people are right handed; irrespective of handedness the left hemisphere is usually the one primarily responsible for speech.[1] The hemispheres are joined by a number of commisures (i.e., sheets of tissue) the most important of which is the *corpus callosum*.

Although the cerebrum comprises two hemispheres the brain is a single functioning unit, in which higher and lower structures are interdependent. In the brain stem is a network of cells called the *reticular formation*, which is of great importance in maintaining alertness: this was isolated in 1949 by Moruzzi and Magoun, although its existence had long been suspected. Impulses go upwards from this formation to the cortex, where activity is organised. Injury to the brain stem causes permanent stupor, as the cerebrum cannot be activated, whereas injury to the cerebrum results in disorganisation of the brain's electrical activity, accompanied by disorganisation of behaviour. Recent clinical and experimental studies of the effect of cutting the corpus callosum suggest that the hemispheres continue to function more or less independently, making it difficult for the individual to integrate his experience. The left hemisphere seems to be primarily responsible for verbal performance, the right for sensori-motor performance (Gazzaniga, Sperry).

The cerebral cortex is of the greatest importance in the control of conscious behaviour. In the history of evolution the sense of smell appears to have been of the greatest importance to the more primitive creatures. As other senses became of greater importance to the higher creatures a new type of cortical tissue appeared, without olfactory functions. If we examine creatures in their phylogenetic sequence we find the first signs of this new tissue, or *neocortex* (as opposed to the *paleocortex* of simple vertebrates like fish) in birds, and the amount increases as we ascend the phylogenetic scale. In man the amount of cerebral cortex is so great that, if it could be unfolded and laid flat, it would cover the area of a small table cloth. To fit into the skull the cortex is greatly folded, and shows ridges and depressions. The ridges are called *gyri*, the depressions *fissures* or *sulci*.

We may think of the cerebral cortex as divided into lobes; the lobes are in pairs because there are two hemispheres. The lobes at the back of the head are called *occipital*, those at the sides are called *temporal*; those on top are the *parietal*; and immediately behind the forehead are the *frontal* lobes. The frontal lobes, which are of particular

---

[1] M. Annett (*Nature*, 1964, vol. 204, pp. 59–60) argues that cerebral dominance is determined genetically, the normal right hander having two dominant genes (DD) for left hemisphere dominance, with a few left handers having two recessive genes (RR) for right hemisphere dominance: most left handers have one gene of each type (DR) and exhibit effects of both genes.

importance in the organisation of conscious actions, are bounded by two fissures; the *Sylvian fissure* below, and the *central sulcus* above. The ridge in front of the central sulcus is called the *precentral gyrus*; the ridge behind the central sulcus is the *post-central gyrus* (see Fig. 11:1).

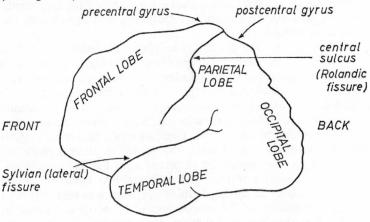

Figure 11:1
General geography of the cerebral cortex.

Our knowledge of the workings of the brain comes from three main sources: experimental studies of animals (mainly rats); clinical studies of patients with brain tumours and injuries; studies of the effects of electrically stimulating the brains of patients undergoing operations for the removal of brain tumours.

With regard to animals there is no need for us to examine the large amount of data under this heading, particularly as Luria (1969) argues that the human cortex is organised in such a way that comparisons with rats are misleading. In particular rats have no frontal lobes to compare with those of human beings. Such studies as have been done (the classical work being by Lashley) have shown decrement in performance to be correlated with the *amount* of tissue destroyed rather than the site of the injury. This does not mean that specific functions, such as vision, hearing, and so on, are not localised in the cerebral cortex; it means that, in addition to specific functions, the cortex acts as a whole in learning.

With regard to the studies of human beings the position is complicated by the fact that lesions are seldom localised, and so one cannot be certain of finding precise connections between brain damage and the resulting effect upon behaviour. However from the work of

L.A.T.I.H.D.—E

surgeons such as Penfield (see Penfield and Roberts) and psychologists such as Luria (1969) the position is becoming clear. Functions are localised, in particular around the central sulcus. The precentral gyrus is the site of the control of many bodily movements; the postcentral gyrus controls sensations. There are other control centres, but the pre- and post-central gyri are particularly important.[1] The frontal lobes do not control sensations and movements, but serve to organise action.

Human beings have the ability to plan their behaviour, and to form strategies for dealing with problems. The higher animals also have this capacity, but it is particularly well developed in man. This view has been developed by Miller, Galanter and Pribram, and is also held by Luria. Luria (1969) discusses many cases of patients with frontal lobe lesions to show how such injury causes the organisation of behaviour to break down. One case is of a soldier with a gunshot wound of the frontal lobes who started to plane a plank but was unable to stop; eventually he planed away half the workbench. Another case is of a woman with a frontal lobe tumour who was one day found to be stirring burning coal with a broom, and who cooked the bristles of the broom instead of noodles. Lesions in places other than the frontal lobes do not result in such bizarre disorganisations of behaviour.

We have mentioned before that Luria believes that language plays a vital role in the control of behaviour, and in Chapter 9 we discussed his illustrations of the use of language to regulate behaviour in young children. Frontal lobe lessions produce the same lack of co-ordination between language and behaviour as that observed in these children. There are two aspects of this regulation by language: the *impellant* function of speech (saying 'go' and pressing a button) and the *analysing* function of mature language which develops after spoken utterance has become internalised. In the early stages of the development of a frontal lobe tumour the analysing function is lost. Later the impellant function may be impaired because, if the patient is required to say 'strong-slight-slight' simultaneously striking the table with one strong knock and two slight ones, he may continue to say 'strong-slight-slight-strong-slight-slight', and find it difficult to stop. This perseveration of behaviour (which we mentioned also in the case of the soldier planing the work bench) is characteristic of certain forms of frontal lobe lesions.

The patients discussed by Luria exhibited loss of speech control

[1] Penfield claims that stimulation of specific points of the temporal cortex activates specific memories in the form of images, which the patient observes as if watching a film.

as one feature of a general loss of organising ability. Luria argues that the suggestion, made at different times by Hebb and by Skinner (1938), that CNS should stand not for '*central* nervous system' but for '*conceptual* nervous system' should be taken literally, because the role of the frontal lobes appears to be to form conceptions of the world and one's place in it. Luria's view of the role played by speech in this process of conceptualising is striking in view of Condillac's argument (see Chapter 2) that man's use of speech was the factor that enabled him to reflect upon his sensory impressions, thus forming ideas of a higher order. (See also Luria, 1959.)

There are other cases of brain damage that result in speech loss without causing a general disorganisation of behaviour, and we must examine these now. The loss of linguistic ability resulting from brain injury is called *aphasia*, and is particularly associated with injuries to the frontal lobe of the left cerebral hemisphere. It occurs commonly among the elderly as a result of strokes, which may be caused by a blood clot circulating in the blood stream (embolism), a fixed clot in a blood vessel (thrombosis), or haemorrhage following rupture of a blood vessel. Characteristically there is an initial complete loss of speech, followed by some improvement as a result of compensatory changes in blood flow giving an enriched supply of blood to areas surrounding the site of the injury. The patient in this improved condition often mispronounces words, or uses the wrong word, or an incorrect part of speech: typically he makes mistakes similar to those of young children learning to talk. Bilingual patients show defects in both languages, but sometimes recovery is greater in one tongue than in the other (Lambert and Fillenbaum; Penfield and Roberts). Some neurologists assert that areas surrounding the site of the injury 'take over' the function of the damaged region, but it is likely that these areas originally played a minor role in speech production but now play a major role. After this initial improvement there may be further recovery of the speech function, but recovery is seldom complete in adults. In the case of children under ten years of age there is a process of relearning, i.e., the child goes again through the developmental sequence described in Chapter 2. This suggests that the original plasticity of the brain is lost as the individual grows older.[1]

[1] At birth the hemispheres seem to be equipotential so if one is damaged the other develops control of language, but dominance of one hemisphere (usually the left) appears after 20 months and increases until the teens, by which time it is fairly firmly established. On Annett's model the chances of recovery from aphasia are largely dependent upon the individual's genetic makeup. See footnote on p. 128.

We have spoken of aphasia as language loss resulting from brain injury, but the clinical picture is more complicated than this formulation may suggest. Aphasias may be sensory (receptive) or motor (expressive); in sensory aphasia the patient cannot interpret sensory signals, in motor aphasia he cannot make the appropriate movements that enable him to communicate linguistically. The language loss may be in the area of speech, or in the areas of reading and writing. The inability to write is called *agraphia*, the inability to read being called *alexia*. (The developmental disability to read encountered in some children is called *dyslexia*; it is an open question whether this is the result of a neurological defect.) Penfield (Penfield and Roberts) reports that the four types of defect are connected and that it is rare to find one without the others, although one type may predominate in an individual patient. Many names have been proposed for defects of varying degrees of specificity, but as the details are not crucial to an understanding of the overall picture we shall not discuss them here. There is, in any case, evidence to suggest that the clinical picture is misleading, and that linguistic deficit in aphasia is a unitary defect, asphasic 'types' representing degrees of loss exhibited by patients with illnesses of varying degrees of severity, or examined at different stages of recovery (Schuell and Jenkins).

Penfield believes that aphasic disturbance arises not directly from the death of brain tissue but from the malfunctioning of tissue surrounding the site of injury. This might help to account for the many reported cases of brain injury that have no appreciable immediate behavioural or intellectual effect. One of the most dramatic cases occurred in 1848 when Phineas T. Gage, working on the Rutland and Burlington Railroad, had an iron bar driven by an explosion in through one temple and out at the other. The bar was three foot seven inches long and one and a quarter inches in diameter, and landed some yards away. Gage exhibited some convulsive movements of his limbs, but was able to talk to his workmates, who put him on an ox cart and drove him three-quarters of a mile to hospital. There, with a little assistance he walked up a long flight of stairs. Subsequently, when disease set in around the injured parts of the brain, he lost consciousness and become delirious, but he eventually recovered (see Beekman for discussion of this case).[1] The most significant aspect of the case from our point of view is that the lesion did not cause aphasia. However, many cases have been reported in

[1] Reports vary as to the precise route taken by the bar, but the frontal lobes appear to have been damaged. After recovering Gage had a markedly changed personality, exhibiting the loss of control over orderly behaviour characteristic of frontal lobe injury.

which very small lesions are associated with impairment, so the site of the injury is clearly of very great importance.

The controversy over the localisation of functions in the cerebral cortex was a lively one in the nineteenth century. In the early part of the century Gall had urged, on pragmatic grounds rather than a thorough understanding of anatomical principles, that different regions of the brain controlled different faculties (faculties of sagacity, amatoriness, and so on). Gall's pupil, Spurzheim, developed this idea into the notion that the faculties could be detected by feeling bumps on the head, corresponding to the brain contours beneath. This idea was complete nonsense, which in no way prevented the doctrine of phrenology not only from becoming a commercial success with the sale of charts of bumps, reproductions of heads of famous men and so on, but also being seriously discussed as the basis of pedagogy. Among many scientists, however, phrenology encountered scorn, which disposed neurologists to discountenance the belief in cortical localisation (see Temkin). The work of Fritsch and Hitzig in 1870 finally established that control of specific functions was localised in the cortex, and their work was dubbed 'the new phrenology'.

With particular reference to the localisation of speech functions one of the most celebrated observations was made in 1861 by Paul Broca, a surgeon at the Bicêtre Hospital in Paris, at a post-mortem examination that he carried out on a patient who for years before his death had exhibited severe speech loss. Broca identified the posterior part of the third left frontal convolution of the cerebral cortex as the area responsible, and this has ever since been known as 'Broca's area'. In 1874, following the work of Fritsch and Hitzig, Wernicke reported the case of a patient with sensory, rather than motor, aphasia. Wernicke identified the area responsible as lying in the first convolution of the *temporal* rather than the frontal lobe. Many investigations since have shown that linguistic ability has many different aspects, probably with different localisations. (For the views of an early critic of Broca and Wernicke see Cole; for a general account see Goldstein; for the history of the subject see Penfield and Roberts, ch. 4, and Riese, 1947. See also Fig. 11:2.)

One factor contributing to the difficulty of assessing the findings is the lack of an appropriate analysis of aphasia from the linguistic point of view. So far we have been using the terms 'speech loss' and 'language loss' almost interchangeably. This is because the workers in the field of neurology talk sometimes of speech and sometimes of language as if the two were identical. The evidence does suggest a generalised disturbance of the symbolic activity that we call 'linguistic', which is, of course, expressed through speech, but a number of cases suggest that closer analysis might contribute much. One case discussed by Toulmin (1968) illustrates the point clearly. The case (reported by Geschwind and Fusillo) was of a patient who had lost the ability to name colours. When asked 'what colour are bananas?' he could reply 'bananas are yellow', but he could not supply the word 'yellow' as the name of a colour in isolation. In what precise way had the patient 'lost' colour names?

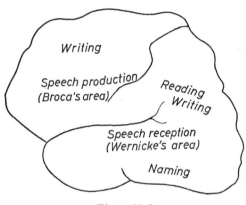

Figure 11:2
Localisation of linguistic functions in the cortex.

One source of the difficulty in answering such questions is that patients are seldom able to describe their own symptoms articulately. A notable exception is the case of Jacques Lordat, reported and discussed by Riese (1954). Lordat was a physician who suffered a transient aphasia at the age of fifty-two. On recovery he described his symptoms. At first he was unable to find the correct expressions, his disability increasing rapidly until about twenty-four hours later he could utter only a few words. Lordat reported that inwardly he could arrange his thoughts and construct lectures, but he was unable to hold even the simplest everyday conversations. Moreover he was unable to read. He also reported that, when he began to recover, he employed the wrong word, knowing it to be wrong. This is character-istic of patients recovering from strokes. From the present point of view the question is the precise nature of Lordat's linguistic loss. If he could arrange his thoughts in lecture form but could not utter them, how much of the linguistic function was lost?

One must be cautious in interpreting the Lordat case, as it may not have been true aphasia. The transient nature of the case, and the ability that Lordat reports of being able to arrange his thoughts with customary facility whilst being unable to express them, suggest two possibilities: either an hysterical condition brought on by over-work and emotional upset, i.e., what is vaguely termed a 'nervous breakdown'; or a temporary condition affecting the medulla, which is the part of the myelencephalon directly connected to the spinal cord. These possibilities have been discussed by Bay.

Another important question that an analysis of aphasic defect might answer concerns patients who, being congenitally deaf, never develop speech, but learn to communicate by gestures. When such patients have strokes, what is the nature of their aphasic defect? Very few cases have been reported, but they have recently been discussed by Sarno *et al.,* who add a description of a case of their own. As their own case is the most clearly reported we shall describe it as probably representative of the others.

Their patient was a congenitally deaf man, born of deaf parents and with deaf siblings. Although he could articulate he communi-cated by finger-spelling and sign language. In finger-spelling each letter is indicated by a finger, and the patient points to the fingers in turn to build up a word; in sign language a gesture is used to re-present a word or phrase. Following his stroke the patient's use of both modes of communication was affected, finger-spelling more so than sign language.

The importance of an analysis of aphasic defect from a linguistic point of view has been stressed by Lenneberg (1960). Early attempts at a linguistic analysis of aphasia are discussed by Marx, but as these attempts are of historical interest only we shall not summarise them in detail. Two views are of particular interest from this period: Hughlings Jackson argued that patients had not lost words as such, but the ability to employ words in propositions; Henry Head regarded aphasia as a disturbance of the power to formulate and express thoughts symbolically. As Lenneberg points out it is not symbolic function as such that is disturbed, as many aphasic patients can interpret direction signs such as a pointing finger without being able to use language. We would agree with Lenneberg that an analysis of symbolic function is called for. In terms of the analysis offered in the first chapter of this book it appears that the cases described by Lenneberg exhibit disturbance of *discursive* symbolism but not of *representational* symbolism. (We should note that the patient des-cribed by Sarno *et al.* had disturbance of discursive symbolism, although he lacked speech and communicated in signs and gestures. For this patient gestures were the normal mode of discursive ex-pression. We shall take up this point again later.)

One linguist who has discussed aphasia as a linguistic problem is Jakobson, who draws attention to two modes of figurative expression: metaphor and metonymy. In metaphor we employ expressions based on similarity, e.g., 'he has a heart of stone'; in metonymy the expressions are based upon contiguity, e.g., 'he is on the bottle', where 'bottle' stands for the alcohol that it contains. Aphasics suffer from deterioration of one rather than the other mode of expression, or if both modes are disturbed one exhibits greater disturbance than the other. An aphasic who has lost the ability to deal in similarities will be unable to find synonyms, and will respond to a request to give another word for a well-known object by giving a response suggested by contiguity. Thus to the question 'what is champagne?' he might reply 'hangover'. An aphasic suffering from the opposite disorder (disturbance of the contiguity function) presents the case of regression to infant speech. Such a patient will have difficulty in distinguishing different suffixes, and will tend to confuse such words as 'jewel', 'jeweller', and 'jewellery'.

Important in Jakobson's analysis is the notion of verbal context, discussed in Chapter 3. The normal speaker can both understand words from their contexts and invent new contexts in order to discuss words themselves. The aphasic patient is disturbed in one or other of these skills. This view is in line with the well-known observation that patients with brain injury are unable to deal in abstractions, whether the task is presented verbally or in the form of blocks of different shapes and sizes to be sorted into categories.[1] (This disability has been particularly emphasised by Goldstein.) With particular regard to the examples presented earlier for discussion it could explain the Geschwind and Fusillo case if we allow that the question 'what colour are bananas?' provided a context in which the patient could answer 'bananas are yellow', whereas the request to name a colour in the abstract provided no context. In general, however, it is difficult to see how this linguistic analysis helps us to understand the problem of aphasia. This is not to say that linguistic analysis may not eventually prove helpful, but it does not appear to clarify many problems at present.

The case of patients lacking language as a result of congenital deafness suggests that an analysis of the symbolic function may usefully precede a linguistic analysis. We have more than once made use of Langer's distinction of two forms of symbolism: discursive and (as we put it) representational. Langer argues that the ability to represent the world symbolically is inherent in our perceptual activity, and that we perceive an object simultaneously as a thing in

[1] As in the Semeonoff–Vigotsky test (see Chapter 9).

its own right and as representative of a class. (Piaget's example of his young daughter encountering a slug when out for a walk is very relevant here. Her father pointed out the slug, then a little further on they came across another. Piaget asked his daughter 'is it the same slug?' and she said that it was. They went back and looked at the other slug, but his daughter continued to maintain that it was the same slug. She was trying to express the idea of 'another of the same type' but had not yet been able to extract the concept of 'slug' of which the two slugs encountered were exemplars.) Langer's chief concern is with the perception of meaningful forms, which was a major concern of the early development of the gestalt school. The problem facing this school can be illustrated with reference to a triangle. When we see a triangle it has a shape, and is not just a collection of lines: we perceive the lines and the shape, so that when we see another triangle we recognise it as a triangle. However, it is unlikely that the two triangles will be identical in all respects, so what is this 'shape' that we have perceived. One school of thought argued that there are no shapes, but that we impose meaning on the universe; but the gestalt psychologists insisted that shapes were as much a part of the universe as the features recorded by physical instruments. This is the view supported by Langer. Symbols for Langer are the organism's way of recording the perceptual world.

This doctrine is partly psychological and partly philosophical. The doctrine that shapes exist independently of perception is an epistemological doctrine of some dubiety, which was formulated to oppose the even more dubious doctrine that our symbolic view of the universe is an arbitrary construction, and that only the data of physics are real. From a psychological point of view the most that can safely be said is that we encode sensory data in such a way as to form representations of the universe, which enable us to operate effectively in the world around us. Evidence from studies of brain pathology suggests that the frontal lobes are particularly important in this respect, and that man's possession of the discursive power of language (which normally takes the form of speech but which, as we saw in the case of the congenitally deaf patient, may take the form of gestures) enables him to operate far more effectively than other creatures.

PART THREE
Philosophical Perspective

I 2

QUESTIONS OF MEANING

This book is by a psychologist and is intended primarily as a psychological work. Psychology, however, sprang from philosophy, and there are many topics of common interest to psychologists and philosophers, important among which is the question of meaning. We shall look briefly at the work of some philosophers on this topic to see what light it can shed upon the interests of psychologists before examining the contributions of psychologists themselves.

Possibly the first philosopher to discuss the topic in a way that is of psychological interest was Charles Peirce, the nineteenth-century American philosopher associated with the philosophical doctrine of pragmatism. Nearer our own time Ogden and Richards published a number of papers in the early part of this century, these being collected and published as *The Meaning of Meaning* in 1923. The title seems a little old-fashioned today, when philosophers are less inclined to ask questions about the 'meaning' of abstract terms (the current practice is to ask not what a word means but how it is used) but the book is valuable in discussing the nature of signs. A particular danger to which the use of signs can lead is *reification*, i.e., assuming that because we have a name for a concept the concept has substantive existence. (A fascinating supplement by Crookshank illustrates how doctors may be misled into inaccurate classification of diseases because various symptoms have been grouped into inadequate diagnostic categories.) Ogden and Richards insist that a symbol, such as a word, is connected with the thought for which it stands, and this thought is connected with exemplars of the thought, but the word and the exemplar are not directly connected. Thus the word *dog* symbolises my concept of 'dog', and an actual dog is an exemplar of my concept of dog. I may say that the word *dog* 'stands for' examples of dogs that I see, so long as I do not suppose that it is directly connected with these dogs. To suppose this would lead one into such difficulties as asking how one word can symbolise so many diverse specimens. The relationships between reference, referent, and symbol are shown in Fig. 12:1, which is a modification of the figure given by Ogden and Richards.

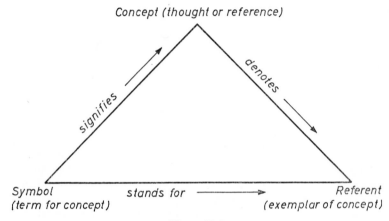

Figure 12:1

Relations between reference, symbol, and referent
(after Ogden and Richards).

A more recent contribution to the philosophy of meaning, following the work of Russell and Wittgenstein, was made in a very influential work by Ayer, who is concerned to discuss meaning and metaphysics. Philosophy has been traditionally thought of as concerned with metaphysics, but Ayer considers metaphysics to be nonsense and wishes to banish it from his philosophy. To balance this negative aim he has the positive aim of formulating a theory of meaning (based upon logic) as a basis for the new philosophy.

For Ayer metaphysics is composed of statements that are not literally meaningful, i.e., they are neither true in virtue of the meanings of the terms of which they are composed (e.g., 'all brothers are male' in which 'being male' is part of the connotation of 'brother') nor are they factual statements that can, at least in principle, be submitted to empirical test. The ability to see how one could put a statement to the test is very important in this philosophy, because if there were no conceivable conditions under which a statement could be tested, we should have to regard the statement as not being a factual one. Moreover, the conditions under which one puts a statement to the test define its meaning. Thus by 'There is a chair on the other side of that door' I mean 'If you go through that door you will see a chair.' This is the meaning of the statement whether or not a chair is found, i.e., the meaning of a statement is the same irrespective of its truth or falsity. The meaning lies not in actually verifying the statement but in the means used to attempt to verify it.

There has been much debate in linguistic philosophical circles about the meaning of terms such as 'sentence,' 'statement', 'proposition', and even 'word'. This debate is associated with the names of Austin and Wittgenstein. As it is lengthy we can only pick out the main conclusions as stated by Ayer. A *sentence* is any form of words that is grammatically significant. A sentence that indicates something, whether or not it is literally meaningful (according to the two criteria already given in the previous paragraph) expresses a *statement*. Statements that are literally meaningful express *propositions*.

We have seen that the two criteria for meaningfulness of propositions are that a proposition must be true in virtue of the terms composing it (in which case we call it 'analytic') or that it be empirically verifiable in principle. The description 'empirically verifiable in principle' means that we must be able to look for some evidence relevant to the truth or falsity of the proposition. The question that we must resolve concerns the meaning of 'relevant' in this context. We have given above an example of a proposition ('There is a chair on the other side of that door') that can be verified (or falsified) by the *direct* means of going through the door to look; but what should we make of propositions such as 'There is a skeleton of a mammoth inside that mountain', if the mountain in question were one that it was impossible to enter? The proposition is meaningful because we can say 'If you *could* enter the mountain you *would* find the skeleton of a mammoth'. This proposition would be *indirectly* verifiable.

Verifiability can refer to a range of observations. In the example of the chair one could see it, touch it, or stumble over it. We might also be in error; we might, for example, have an hallucination of seeing a chair. These points are irrelevant to the fact that, in going in search of the chair, we are seeking evidence relevant to determining the truth or falsity of the proposition. It is the conceivability of seeking relevant evidence that makes a proposition meaningful.

We have already mentioned (Chapter 4) that Ayer believes metaphysical statements to have arisen because of a misuse of language, and it is certainly true that language sometimes seems to take on a life of its own. As an example Ayer quotes the following: 'the

Absolute enters into, but is itself incapable of, evolution and progress'. Such statements appear to express something, but when we examine them we find that they are neither analytic nor empirically verifiable: no conceivable evidence would be relevant to determining the truth or falsity of the statement about the Absolute.

If philosophy is not to be concerned with metaphysical speculations, what is to be its function? Ayer considers that the function of philosophy is to be wholly critical, to consider, for example, such topics as when a conclusion deduced from evidence can be regarded as rational. This is not the same as asking whether the conclusion is true or false, but is a question of deciding what is meant by 'rational' in a given set of circumstances. This is not a scientific question, but a linguistic one, so philosophy does not compete with science.

In Chapter 4 we said that much confusion had arisen because Indo-European sentences have a *subject–predicate* construction, which misled people into supposing that a predicate always referred to an attribute. If this is a source of confusion it is necessary for the philosopher to offer an alternative analysis of propositions to that in terms of subject and predicate. This was a problem that exercised Bertrand Russell, who proposed as a solution the theory of 'definite descriptions'. It may be illustrated by the sentence 'The present King of France is wise'. There is no King of France, but the sentence is certainly not devoid of meaning, so of whom are we speaking when we say '. . . is wise'? We may reformulate the sentence as 'There is a person of whom it is true that he and only he is King of France and that he is wise'. This statement can be seen to be false. This reformulation gets us out of the dilemma of a subject-predicate analysis, according to which the statement 'The present King of France is wise' is either meaningless or else there is a King of France, about whom the statement is either true or false. (See Strawson, ch. 6, for further discussion.)

The difficulties raised by the use of language led Russell to prefer the mathematical symbolism, worked out by himself in conjunction with Whitehead in *Principia Mathematica*, for the discussion of problems of this sort. We need not deal with this development of philosophy, as our aim is to demonstrate the difficulties involved in the philosophical analysis of language.

One example given by Ayer is of particular interest to us. Consider the two sentences: 'He is the author of that book' and 'A cat is a mammal'. The first of these sentences means 'He and no one else wrote that book', the second means 'The class of mammals contains the class of cats'. The word 'is' thus has more than one meaning. The fact that a symbol can have more than one meaning poses considerable problems for psychologists attempting to account for a child's learning the meaning of words.

To illustrate the attempt we may consider the views of Mowrer, which involve the concept of mediating responses, introduced in Chapter 7. This concept originated with the work of Hull and was developed by Osgood among others. The account given in Chapter 7 was based on the ideas of Maltzman, which differ in some respects from those of Osgood. We shall not discuss here the technical differences between the various accounts, but shall pick out the essential features of the mediation hypothesis on which Mowrer's account is based.

Stimuli elicit responses. However, both stimuli and responses are complex. An electric shock will elicit the response of withdrawing a limb, but it will also cause anxiety. If the shock is accompanied by a buzzer, the buzzer will elicit anxiety, so the anxiety reaction becomes detached from the shock situation; i.e., the sound of a buzzer will tend to elicit anxiety even when no shock is likely to follow, so the buzzer is acting as a sign that an unpleasant stimulus may follow. Over a period of time the anxiety may become minimal, and take the form of alertness to the possibility of danger. In this way a system of signs is built up, some of which derive from innate response tendencies, whilst others originate in contingent learning situations. This postulated mechanism of the development of signs is regarded as particularly important by Morris (Morris, 1946), and is the basis of Mowrer's theory of language.

In a wide-ranging paper published in 1954 (see also Mowrer, 1960) Mowrer discusses many aspects of the psychology of language, including the possibility that language serves primarily to convey meaning. It is this aspect of Mowrer's paper that is of particular interest to us here. Mowrer argues that when two people communicate they must have in common a system of signs, upon whose meanings they agree, and that communication involves changing meaning from one sign to another. Thus if A tells B that 'Tom is a thief', A is informing B that the meaning of the word 'thief' (which both know) is to be attached to 'Tom' (whom they both know). By the principle of conditioning B will now respond to the word 'Tom' in the way that he previously responded to the word 'thief'. The mechanism is that by which Pavlov's dogs came to salivate to the sound of a bell, which had been associated with the presence of food, because the bell had come to have the same meaning for the dogs as the food previously had.

One objection to the theory as presented so far is that it would appear to make the words 'Tom' and 'thief' synonymous, which is clearly not the case. To overcome this objection Mowrer proposes that the name 'Tom' produces in the hearer a range of responses, including various sensations, and that the reactions to the word 'thief' become conditioned to just part of the range of responses to 'Tom'. We can add that not all the reactions to 'thief' are elicited by the situations (i.e., the hearer will not immediately call 'stop thief' or call a policeman) but characteristically only the feeling of repugnance will be aroused. We have the case of part of the response to the name 'Tom' becoming linked to part of the response to the word 'thief'. This is an instance of a mediating response, as defined above. (For convenience of reference we may use the symbol r_m to stand for 'mediating response').

Mowrer put forward this view in what he called an 'exploratory' way, inviting scholars from other disciplines to discuss it from the standpoints of their respective disciplines. Among those who have done so is Fodor, who points out that, in the first place, the account lacks generality. For instance, in the sentence 'Tom is a perfect idiot' the meaning is a function of the parts of the sentence; we cannot suppose that the meanings of both 'idiot' and 'perfect' have become attached to 'Tom', because in this case the adjective 'perfect' qualifies not 'Tom' but 'idiot'. Even more serious is the fact that Mowrer's explanation does not account satisfactorily even for the example given, because it relies upon the dubious assumption that a name and a predicate are the same type of word. That they are not is suggested by the fact that we can ask 'Who is Tom?' but not 'Who is thief'? Moreover we can ask 'What does "thief" mean?' whilst it would be strange to ask 'What does "Tom" mean?'

One difference between names and predicates lies in the different circumstances in which they are learned. One learns the name of a person called Tom by hearing the word spoken when he is pointed out, or in general terms when the name is uttered (in speech or writing) when he is indicated (by demonstration or description). Mowrer suggests that the meanings of predicates are learned in the same way, but Fodor points out that few people learn the meaning of the word 'thief' by hearing it spoken in the presence of actual thieves. Instead the ways in which the meaning of a predicate can be learned are considerably more varied than those in which the names of people can be learned.

One other difficulty of this theory relates to words like 'dragons', 'elves', and 'unicorns'. A child may understand perfectly the meaning of the sentence 'unicorns are nasty' but we cannot suppose that the child must have been in the presence of unicorns in order to understand the sentence. The fact is that words may signify things without denoting anything (in Fig. 12:1, the left-hand arm may be present without the right-hand arm), which raises difficulties for a theory of meaning ba ed upon the principles of conditioning. One could argue that part of the meaning of horse becomes attached to part of the meaning of horn to form the notion of a unicorn, but it is difficult to see how this process could be explained by a theory that accounts for associative learning in terms of the reinforcement of connections.

Indeed the notion of reinforcement is seen by Fodor as one of the major objections to $S-R$ theory. We saw in Chapter 2 that one of Chomsky's objections to Skinner's account of verbal learning was that it failed to account for the child's capacity to understand, as well as to produce, sentences never previously uttered in his presence, and Fodor argues that Mowrer's account, although more sophisticated in some respects than Skinner's, is open to the same objection. (See also Katz and Fodor.)

A further difficulty of the theory is that it does not account for disbelieving what one is told. If it were the case that I react to 'Tom' as I react to 'thief', then on being told 'Tom is a thief' I should take anti-theft precautions. If I do not believe that Tom is a thief I take no such precautions, in other words I do not react to Tom as to a thief; I have nevertheless understood the meaning of 'Tom is a thief'.

Perhaps the most serious difficulty of the mediation hypothesis account of meaning arises from the fact that stimuli and responses are seldom unique in all respects, but typically have features in common. The common features of stimuli S_1 and S_2 will be ab-abstracted by the subject as s. Let us say that S_1 commonly produces response R_1 and that S_2 produces R_2. If R_1 and R_2 have a common feature r, then the mediation hypothesis would lead us to expect a connection to be developed between s and r. Let us represent the situation as in Fig. 12:2. From Fig. 12:2 we see that either S_1 or S_2 could give rise, via the $s-r$ link, to either R_1 or R_2 (see Chapter 7). Now if words acquire meanings through association with stimuli, then the mediation hypothesis account cannot explain the fact that a word will have one meaning rather than another. The explanation will by itself be necessary but not sufficient. To overcome the difficulty one must postulate a further connection between every mediating response and the meaning that is attached to it. However, if we do this we remove the only advantage that the mediation hypothesis possesses, because we are postulating a set of one-to-one connections between stimuli and responses. A theory based upon one-to-one connections has great difficulty in explaining the flexibility of language, and it was to overcome this difficulty that the mediation hypothesis account was formulated.

In the light of these criticisms it may be thought that neither the *S–R* theory of Skinner nor the mediation hypothesis account of Mowrer has much to offer psychology. To take this view, however, would be to suppose too much. It was said in Chapter 2 that a psychologist of a behaviourist inclination would accept that the behaviourist account of an abstruse problem like meaning has many flaws, but would insist that the attempt to apply this approach was

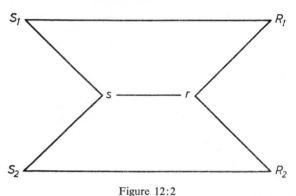

Figure 12:2
The place of a mediating response in an S-R connection.

valid. It is easy to see what the difficulties are, but it is not easy to see that the critics have a better explanation to offer. Fodor's criticism of Mowrer certainly illuminates the problem, but neither in the paper referred to, nor in the paper on the structure of semantic theory (Katz and Fodor) which shows the relevance of the deep structure and transformation rules discussed in Chapter 2 to an analysis of the difficulties, does the linguistic approach contribute any more than the behaviourist approach to their solution.

Before leaving the problem of meaning we must mention the work of Osgood, Suci, and Tannenbaum, which offers some support to the mediation hypothesis, and suggests a possible way of meeting Fodor's objection that the mediation hypothesis fails to postulate a sufficient, as well as a necessary, cause in the learning of meanings, at least with regard to words. The most important feature of their work in the present connection concerns the *semantic differential*, which is a technique for specifying the meaning that a word has for an individual.

In essence the technique involves asking a subject to rate, on a

7-point scale, various bipolar qualities of a word. Thus a subject may be asked to rate the word 'mother' for possession of the quality of angularity or roundness, giving a rating of 7 to the meaning 'extremely angular' and 1 to 'extremely rounded'. He is then asked to repeat the judgement for the qualities 'good – bad', 'tense – relaxed', and so on. Although this may sound a bizarre experiment, subjects have no difficulty in performing the task. As a result a profile of the judgements may be drawn, as in Fig. 12:3.

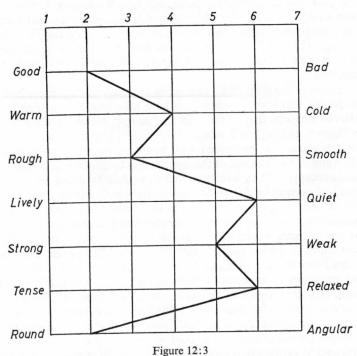

Figure 12:3

Hypothetical semantic profile of the word 'mother'.

The fact that it is possible to exercise judgements of this type suggests that subjective meaning involves the abstraction of common properties from different words: indeed, studies have shown that there are three major factors involved in the subjective meanings of words, namely, *activity* (e.g., fast – slow, active – passive, excitable – calm); *potency* (e.g., hard – soft, masculine – feminine, strong – weak); and *evaluation* (e.g., good – bad, kind – cruel, beautiful – ugly). However the fact that these can be quantitatively distinguished suggests that it may be possible, at least in principle, to specify the uniqueness of verbal mediating responses whose absence from Mowrer's account was noted by Fodor.

Gombrich (1963) interprets Osgood's work as suggesting that human beings have a tendency to classify complex meanings in terms of simple sensory responses. In his own work Gombrich (1960) has shown that the most diverse phenomena can be dichotomised into ping and pong. For instance, most people will say that a mouse is a ping and an elephant a pong, but Gombrich goes further by comparing a work by Klee with one by Kandinsky on the same theme, suggesting convincingly that the Kandinsky is a pong and the Klee a ping. The implications of this analysis would seem to be that sensory qualities of words and experiences contribute directly to meaning.

In view of the difficulties inherent in the study of meaning it is not surprising that some psychologists have attempted to construct theories of language that do not refer to meaning. Notable among these is Skinner, although as Toulmin (1968) points out, Skinner himself is relatively cautious compared with some of his students, such as Holz and Azrin. The aim of this approach is to dispense with mentalistic concepts such as intention, and to explain language entirely in terms of operant behaviour and reinforcement. Toulmin argues that the Skinnerian approach can best be understood as a reaction to the outmoded philosophy that regarded meaning as a private entity akin to mental images which are available only to introspection. The revolution in philosophy brought about by Wittgenstein has dispensed with the mental image theory of meaning, preferring to derive the meanings of expressions from the contexts in which they are used. (Another aspect of this problem is discussed in Chapter 9. For a more extended discussion, by Skinner and others, see Wann.)

The Skinnerian approach to language makes no distinction between the use of language in context and the speech in which that language is expressed, or, as Toulmin puts it, Holz and Azrin make 'no distinction between language and prattle'. Essentially this approach concentrates upon the superficial aspects of communication in the belief that to talk of deep aspects is meaningless. It may be instructive to compare this approach with that of the prophet of illiteracy Marshall McLuhan. Newton–de Molina (1970) has drawn attention to McLuhan's application to literary criticism of information theory. As we pointed out in Chapter 3 information theory is concerned with the transmission of messages irrespective of sense, so to discuss communication in terms of information theory amounts to regarding the content of a message as of precisely the same importance as the modality in which it is expressed. Thus Skinner may be regarded as the McLuhan of psychology (or McLuhan as the Skinner of literary criticism, depending upon whether one wishes to bury Caesar or to praise him, and upon whom one regards as Caesar[1]).

Much confusion appears to have arisen from a failure to distinguish *language* from *speech*. When a man uses language he employs symbols, which usually take the form of speech, but his language is much more than the symbols: as has been made clear in previous chapters it includes the rules of syntax and semantic reference. When one reads the behaviourists one often has the impression that they are using the term 'linguistic behaviour' as co-terminus with 'the production of words'. Since, however, language is not just words, but the organisation and arrangement of words, it would appear that language and 'linguistic behaviour' are in different logical categories, requiring different approaches. One might object that 'behaviour in general' is more than just 'responses and movements', but that behaviourism studies the former by way of the latter. In reply one might say that this methodology is probably the crucial weakness of behaviourism, which is revealed more clearly in its application to language than to any feature of nonhuman activity. We may retain the term 'linguistic behaviour' for ease of reference, but to imagine that, by substituting this term for the wider term 'language' we can apply the methods of the animal laboratory to the study of articulate speech, is to exhibit a degree of naivety of which, as Koch somewhere remarks, only the most intelligent are capable.

[1] For another discussion of McLuhan see Wagner, ch. 2.

EXPLANATIONS OF LINGUISTIC ABILITY

Man's possession of language makes him unique, but it also appears to cause him concern. Language has been traditionally (if sometimes figuratively) interpreted as a gift from heaven, at least until the behaviourists proposed to interpret it as a highly formalised system of babbling (for a history of views on language see Marx's appendix in Lenneberg, 1967), but is is undeniable that animals do not possess it. The folklore of many countries has tales of animals that can speak, usually once a year, the occasion in Christian countries being Christmas Eve. This suggests that people would like animals to be able to speak, as this would reduce man's feeling of alarm at his own uniqueness; this may help to account for the strenuous efforts made to rear apes in human homes in the hope they would develop speech like human children. Two of the best known of these efforts were made by the Kellog and Hayes families. Neither family succeeded in socialising its pet chimpanzee, and the Hayes family eventually lived in a house with barred windows, ripped curtains, and shabby furniture: in fact, far from their raising their chimpanzee to human living standards, their pet had reduced them to a standard of living approximating that of apes in zoo cages. No one has yet taught an animal to use language. The most that has been achieved is to teach a chimpanzee to produce sounds recognisable as three separate monosyllabic words, but without the ability to put them in correct syntactical order to form a sentence (according to Roger Brown, at a lecture at Edinburgh University in May 1970).

Miller has listed the fact that the ability to use articulate speech is an essentially human characteristic as one of his 'preliminaries to psycholinguistics' (Miller, 1965). This point has been elaborated by

Lenneberg (1964, 1967) who bases his argument on five main considerations. First, verbal behaviour is related to morphological and functional specialisations, particularly in the brain (see Chapter 11). Second, the onset and development of speech in children follow a universal pattern; disease can delay the onset without affecting the maturational sequence (see Chapter 2). Third, the severest handicaps, such as congenital blindness and/or deafness do not prevent children from learning language, although they may, of course, seriously interfere with the production of speech. (Lenneberg does not accept the 'wolf-children' evidence that suggests that children who do not grow up in language communities fail to acquire language, because such evidence is admittedly unreliable – see Lenneberg, 1966. The wittiest discussion of this evidence is by Bergen Evans.) Fourth, language cannot be taught to non-human species, as we have already mentioned. Finally there are universal features of language: e.g., although different languages have different phonemes, the fact is that they all *do* have phonemes; all languages have syntax; and language is used by all men for the purpose of meaningful reference.

The fact that man, whilst part of nature is unique in possessing linguistic ability, raises no difficulty from the biological point of view, as species differentiation (cladogenesis) and change within species (anagenesis) are recognised principles of evolutionary development; and it has been accepted since the early work of Lorenz that the laws of hereditary transmission apply not only to physical structure but to behavioural patterns also (see various papers by Lorenz in Schiller): in short, species uniqueness of behaviour is common in nature. Evidence from patients with various forms of language handicap strongly suggests that language ability is genetically determined in the individual. The argument that man's possession of language is the result of a *qualitative* difference from other creatures, and is not just the result of a quantitatively larger brain, is strengthened by the fact that nanocephalic dwarfs, whose brains when mature rarely exceed in size those of new-born normal infants, nevertheless acquire language to the level of that possessed by normal five-year olds. It seems that the *configuration* of the brain is the important factor, and in particular the development of areas of the cerebral cortex that form associations between the different items of information integrated in other areas (Chase, 1966. For a discussion of relative sizes of the brains of different species see Wilkie, ch. 7).

The evidence is such as to make it reasonably certain that human linguistic ability is an inherited trait, which appeared somewhere in the history of evolution, probably in a humanoid species now extinct, and which may be regarded as part of the connotation of the term 'human'. Let us see what implications this position has for the explanation of human behaviour.

The position may be regarded as 'nativist', as opposed to the 'empiricist' view which seeks to base its explanations of phenomena on learning. The nativist/empiricist controversy has been traditionally associated with the field of perception, where the points at issue have been discussed by many people, for example, Pratt. The heart of the controversy is that, if one wishes to explain human capacities on the basis of learning one has to demonstrate the learning process for innumerable phenomena, whereas if one starts from the assumption that certain features of behaviour are intrinsically human, or animal, or (speaking more generally, are biologically determined) one is relieved of the necessity of accounting for them. This position seems to many people to be unsatisfactory as offering no real explanation.

The role of assumption in scientific explanation has been discussed by Toulmin (1961). He points out that a phenomenon is an unexpected event, which is to be explained. An event can only be unexpected if the scientist has prior expectations, i.e., views of how things naturally are. These views of how things naturally are Toulmin calls 'ideals of natural order'. In the course of time man's views of natural order have changed, and Toulmin illustrates the change with reference to dynamics and to the theory of matter. Aristotle derived his views on dynamics from the observation of everyday occurrences, such as that a stone falls to the ground when dropped, leaving aside hypothetical examples. This meant that he paid little attention to acceleration, which was importantly developed by Galileo. Galileo, from his concern with acceleration, was interested in changes of motion, and his ideal of natural motion was that of a ship sailing on a great circle track around the world. With Newton came a different ideal of motion, namely motion of a body in a straight line, continuing until compelled by force to change its state. With Aristotle, Galileo, and Newton we have three paradigms, or typical cases, in terms of which to view actual cases. In terms of Aristotle's paradigm of bodies naturally coming to rest, the case of a body continuing in circular motion has to be explained, i.e., it is a phenomenon. With Galileo's paradigm of great circle motion, a body coming to rest is a phenomenon. In Newton's system the paradigm is the extremely unlikely case of a body continuing to move in a straight line, and so circular motion is a phenomenon to be explained. Thus some things are taken for granted, others are to be explained. What is taken for granted may be a hypothetical instance of a very high degree of abstraction, as in Newton's case, so that explanation in science is not a question of explaining the unfamiliar in terms of the familiar, but of 'relating the phenomena to the paradigms'. The scientific worth of a paradigm is judged in terms of how many phenomena can be related to it.

The changing relationship of physiology to matter theory illustrates the point that the sciences bear hierarchical relationships to each other, and that their relative positions within the hierarchy may change in the course of time. Thus Aristotle viewed all objects as having a life cycle, which meant that the changes that occur with time in inanimate materials such as metals could be understood by reference to the life cycle of the metal. Even Newton could speculate on the possibility that gold could 'ferment and putrify', but with the development of physical science in the seventeenth and eighteenth centuries, the life-cycle model was discarded in favour of the view that the *constituents* of materials are unchanging. With the rise of this view the physiological model of development was seen to be no longer applicable to the range of phenomena now regarded as the province of physics and chemistry (although the study of viruses and genes suggests that the distinction between animate and inanimate matter is not, after all, absolute).

Psychology appears to be at a stage of paradigmatical development corresponding to Aristotle's views on dynamics. This is no matter for disgrace, because this level of paradigmatical thinking may be the appropriate one for psychology, but many thinkers have attempted to construct abstract models of man in terms of which they seek to explain the natural features of human beings. Attempts to explain the nature of language often seem to regard the state of nonhuman animals as natural, and seek to show how man has come to deviate from this state. If, instead, we regard human abilities, including the capacity for articulate speech, as natural to man, in the same way as it is natural for stones to fall to the ground, we are left with the problem of defining precisely what this nature is. As far as language is concerned we have seen that two explanations have been offered. Chomsky (1968, etc.) argues that we have somehow encoded the principles of 'deep structure' and the accompanying transformational rules, which allow us to recognise as grammatical sentences that we have never heard before, and to generate novel sentences (Chapter 3). Piaget cannot accept the principle of innate encoding but argues instead that actions are co-ordinated according to patterns that can be described mathematically, and this pattern of co-ordination precedes the use of language, which later reflects it (Chapter 10). Inasmuch as Chomsky sometimes writes as if the existence of a given set of grammatical rules describing the organisation of language is less important than the fact that mentality is organised, he is not very far from Piaget. However, Piaget goes further and derives the organisation of mentality from the organisation of nature. It cannot be said that either successfully bridges the lacuna between thought and action, a problem that has exercised man for the whole of his intellectual existence.

One of the major puzzles with regard to thought and language concerns how we know what we are going to say. A sentence proceeds from left to right, but the earlier parts of the sentence are in a sense determined by the later. Thus in the sentence 'I am going to eat my dinner' the idea of dinner must precede the idea of eating, and both must precede the notion that I am about to do something. If this were not so we should be forced to accept the absurd proposition that, like Alice, I could have no idea what I was going to say until I had said it. There is a further problem, viz., having said something how do I know that that was what I intended to say? We have all had the experience of saying something that we did not mean to say, and Freud made use of this observation in his theory of unconscious forces. Aphasic patients, in the process of recovering from strokes, are often very frustrated because they know that what they have said is not what they meant to say. It is reasonable to suppose that, having said something, we can recognise it as what we had it in mind to say, which leaves us with the problem of understanding what we mean by 'having something in mind to say'. This is a very loose way of putting the problem, and anti-mentalists will no doubt find it repugnant, but it probably expresses the problem more satisfactorily than any behaviouristic circumlocution. Since neither behaviourists nor mentalists have any answer to the problem, the mode of formulating it is not at this stage too important.

One point that must be made clear is that it would be wrong to suggest that an actual form of words exists somewhere ready to be spoken. To suppose this would require us to ask where this form of words was before it came into existence, and thus we should be led into an infinite regress. It would be just as wrong to suppose that the meaning of a sentence had an ontological existence distinct from the words composing it and was capable of being discovered: this is the sort of category error discussed by Ryle (ch. 4). It might be thought that linguistics could answer this question with its proposal that 'deep structure' and transformation rules are part of human mentality, and that we learn the words that make it possible to generate sentences on the basis of innate endowment, but this only pushes the problem further back: we have still to explain how it is that we generate one sentence rather than another, and recognise the sentence as one that expresses what we intended to say.

The discussion of intentions is one that has occupied the Oxford linguistic philosophers, and has been concerned with such questions as how one distinguishes an unintentional movement from an intentional movement on epistemological grounds, i.e., what are the appropriate circumstances in which the term 'intentional' is applied. For a discussion of these issues the reader is referred to Hampshire. Since, however, it is a delusion of the linguistic movement to suppose that, once a problem is shown to be improperly formulated it becomes a pseudo-problem and vanishes, in the manner of a snark revealed as a boojum, the approach is not very helpful in dealing with the genuine problem stated in the last paragraph. For this reason we shall omit consideration of this approach, preferring instead to argue by analogy with another puzzling field of human achievement, viz., creative thinking.

The role of the unconscious in creative thinking is well known though poorly understood. Creative thinkers are virtually un-animous in agreeing that a period of conscious preparation must be followed by a period of unconscious intellectual gestation, which is terminated by a flash of insight, after which a further period of conscious work is needed to consolidate the insight. What happens in the unconscious period is a mystery. It may be that various partial hypotheses (deriving from the preparatory period) are put together in different ways until an integration occurs that is recognised as a satisfactory solution of the problem; or alternatively that all possible combinations of ideas are systematically tested, and all but the one found to be satisfactory are erased. Precisely what the unconscious does will probably never be elucidated, for as Piaget says: 'the un-conscious is only the expression of the powerlessness of our intro-spection' (Beth and Piaget, ch. 9). Nevertheless speculation may not be entirely profitless. Applying these speculations to language we have the possibility that, faced with the problem of what to say we unconsciously fit together parts of sentences according to the rules of generative grammar until we formulate one that we recognise as satisfactory; or that we formulate all conceivable sentences within a given range of reference, including those that are ungrammatical, and erase all that are unsatisfactory. Both proposals seem implaus-ible, the second possibly more so than the first, but it is likely that something of this sort happens. The effect of brain damage according to this explanation would be to interfere either with the rapidity of search, or with the power to select the correct formulation and reject all others, or both. Of course, this account does not elucidate the role of the unconscious in language use any more than in creativity, but it may have the heuristic value of directing the search for explanations in the right direction.

The proposed account is consistent with the creative aspect of language use, but there are obvious differences between creative discovery and articulate speech, the most striking being that of speed. If there is an unconscious period between the presentation of an idea and its linguistic expression that period must usually be almost infinitesimally brief, so brief in fact that the model of a search for the expression through all possible formulations seems to be ruled out. However, we should beware of being misled by mechanical models. The objection in terms of lack of time may be conditioned by our knowledge that the time taken in searching, even by the most elaborate computer, is finite. The reply to this objection would not be to demonstrate the possibility of constructing a computer with powers of instantaneous testing and selection, because this would be irrelevant: the computer today has usurped the place in scientific explanatory models held by the telephone exchange in the nineteenth century and clockwork mechanisms in the seventeenth, but our thinking should not always be in the thrall of our technology. (For a discussion of computer models of thinking see Neisser and also Newell, Shaw, and Simon.) We do not know how the brain works, and when we do we may find the explanation in terms of simultaneous search and retrieval not at all implausible. Before Helmholtz measured the velocity of nervous transmission it used to be thought that it was equal to that of light, because that was the only way to account for the speed of thought. Perhaps when we know more about the brain we shall discover that, despite the low speed of transmission of the nerve impulse, the velocity of light is the speed at which the brain conducts its operations.

Let it be clear that we are not postulating a hypothetical mechanism of brain action. Our aim is to characterise the nature of language usage, and to suggest that nothing that we know about brain action makes this characterisation implausible. Postulation of innate mechanisms achieves nothing in the way of explanation. The most that is achieved by these postulations is a characterisation of brain action rather than of observable phenomena, which gives a specious air of scientific rigour whilst directing attention away from the problems to be solved. Whilst agreeing with Hebb that physiology is no sin when publicly recognised we must beware of mistaking appearance for reality.

There has recently been great interest in the potential explanatory power of the postulation of innate mechanisms. From what we have said above it must be clear that we believe the explanatory power of such mechanisms to be a delusion. However, this debate is the culmination of more than three hundred years of Western philosophical thinking, so it may help to obtain a perspective if we give an outline account of the origins of the dispute. This we do in the next chapter.

14

EMPIRICISM AND RATIONALISM

The question of how we are to account for linguistic usage is only one aspect of the general problem of giving an account of nature in general and human nature in particular. As we saw in the previous chapter, the debate is of great antiquity, but when we come to modern times we can take as our starting point the work of the philosopher René Descartes (1596–1650). Descartes eschewed the medieval scholastic approach to philosophical problems, preferring instead to base his reasoning on clear and distinct ideas. In his search for the most certain of these ideas he formulated his celebrated *Cogito, ergo sum* ('I think, therefore I am'). On the basis of clear and distinct ideas Descartes described a scientific methodology in his *Discourse on the Method of Rightly Conducting the Reason and Seeking the Truth in the Sciences* (1637).[1]

Descartes had two major influences. The less important of the two was his influence on the *style* of thinking of his successors, particularly the *philosophes* of the French eighteenth-century Enlightenment. The term *philosophes* is applied to humanistic thinkers whose aim was to solve human problems by an application to human affairs of the powers of reason. They included Condillac, who has been mentioned already (Chapter 2), and Voltaire, who familiarised eighteenth-century France with the writings of the British Empiricists, whose ideas we shall discuss shortly. The *philosophes* and their work are discussed by White.

Descartes' greater influence was on the direction of subsequent philosophical thinking. In arguing that if an idea was so clear and distinct that no man viewing it in the natural light of reason could dispute it, then it must be true, Descartes had raised important

[1] Penguin Books (1968), Ed. J. E. Sutcliffe.

questions about the relationship of the mind to external reality. These were such questions as 'To what extent do we see things as they are?' and 'What is the difference, if any, between visually perceiving objects and mentally perceiving ideas?' and so on. Different views on these questions were taken by the protagonists of empiricism (which explored the explanatory status of sensations arising from interaction with the external world) and rationalism (which investigated the structure of the intellect). The empiricist thinking was established by British philosophers of the seventeenth and eighteenth centuries, the rationalist school by Kant; both viewpoints have their representatives today. We shall first briefly outline the positions of the founding fathers of the schools, then discuss their relevance to the present-day psychology of language.

British empirical philosophy is in one way like an old joke in that it starts with an Englishman, an Irishman, and a Scotsman. These were respectively: John Locke (1632–1704); George Berkeley (1685–1753); and David Hume (1711–76). Hume was the contemporary of the German philosopher Immanuel Kant (1724–1804) to whom we shall return. In this chapter it is possible to treat the ideas of these great men only very briefly; we are less concerned with their philosophy as such than with the importance of their ideas to psychology.

John Locke's most important work was his *Essay Concerning Human Understanding*, published in 1690. In it he argued that a study of philosophy should develop from an understanding of the human mind. His problem was 'epistemology', which tries to answer the question 'How should we talk about the things that we know?' Gilbert Ryle describes the epistemologist's task as drawing logical maps. Locke was the first philosopher to argue that we need to base epistemology on an understanding of the understanding, and he thus paved the way for the development of psychology. He insisted that the child's mind at birth was a blank sheet or *tabula rasa*, on which ideas were impressed through the sensations. In short he held that there are no *innate* ideas, and that we obtain our ideas through sense experience alone.

Like John Locke, Berkeley was concerned with the theory of knowledge. He set out to improve upon Locke, and to remove the confusions caused by other philosophers, who 'raise a dust and then complain that they cannot see'. His major philosophical works were the *New Theory of Vision* (1709) and the *Principles of Human Knowledge* (1710).[1] One source of confusion, Berkeley thought, was a distinction, drawn by Locke, between primary qualities and

[1] Fontana Library (1962), Ed. G. J. Warnock.

secondary qualities. Primary qualities, such as solidity, shape, movement, and number, were held to reside in objects themselves; secondary qualities, such as colours, sounds, tastes, and so on, were added by the mind. Berkeley took the next step and argued that *all* qualities are in the mind.

If all qualities reside in the mind, how do we know that an object is real? We may think we see something but find, when we go to touch it, that no sensation results: in this case we should suppose that we had had a visual hallucination. Suppose, however, that we *had* been able to touch it. We should have had sensations through two separate modalities, but we should still have had only sensations. Therefore, all we mean by saying that something *is*, is that we have perceived it, i.e., to be is to be perceived, or, in Latin, *esse est percipi*. This view is known as 'subjective idealism'.

The last of the British trio was David Hume, whose most important work was *A Treatise on Human Nature* in three volumes, the first two of which appeared in 1739, the third in the following year. The work did not sell as well as Hume had hoped, so in 1748 he published the smaller *Inquiry Concerning the Human Understanding*, which he hoped would make his points clearer. Hume extended Berkeley's subjective idealism to the argument that there is no mind at all, independent of ideas; inasmuch as ideas are caused by sensations, the so-called 'mind' is a congeries of ideas resulting from sensations. This point disturbed Kant, whose major philosophical works were written in opposition to the empirical philosophy.

The British Empiricists, as Wolff points out, 'do not form a school, and their philosophical theories cannot be fitted into a neat progression. Kant, however, seems to have viewed them in this way. He was wrong to do so, but he was not wrong in believing that scepticism and dogmatism (i.e., rationalism) are the natural outgrowths of the Cartesian philosophy'. Let us now briefly examine Kant's reply to empiricism.

Kant's philosophy is called a 'critical philosophy' after his famous *Critique of Pure Reason*, which first appeared in 1781, and later works such as the *Critique of Practical Reason* (1786). Kant attempted to analyse and expound the status of the judgements we make about the things that we believe we know: that is to say, he wanted to answer questions such as: 'What sort of statements do we make when we express judgements? – What sort of statements are they? – What are they about?' Kant's work may be regarded as an attempt to formulate the rules that our judgements must follow if they are to be valid.

Hume had taken the view that our judgements are of two sorts:

either they amplify our knowledge of empirical matters, in which case they can be assessed by reference to evidence; or else they are explicative of the meanings of words (e.g., 'all brothers are male'), in which case they add nothing to the content of our knowledge. At the end of the *Inquiry* Hume had written 'If we take in our hand any volume of divinity or school metaphysics, for instance, let us ask, *Does it contain any experimental reasoning concerning matter of fact and existence*? No. Commit it then to the flames, for it can contain nothing but sophistry and illusion'. Kant accepted and enlarged upon the distinction between two sorts of judgement, but he was unable to go along with Hume in rejecting metaphysics on the grounds that it was not based upon empirical demonstration. In his *Prolegomena to any Future Metaphysics that Will be Able to Represent Itself as a Science* (1783)[1] Kant attempted to put metaphysics on a sure foundation: in doing so he attacked an important tenet of empiricist thinking, namely the belief that there are no innate ideas.

Put very briefly the problem that Kant wished to solve was as follows: are there any judgements that depend upon empirical reasoning for their truth, but which, once having been established are recognised as inevitably true? Judgements whose validity must be established empirically Kant called *synthetic*. Judgements whose truth is independent of empirical evidence, and which are thus inevitably true, Kant called *a priori*. The question may thus be rephrased: 'are there *synthetic a priori* judgements?' Kant believed that there were, and that they were the proper concern of metaphysics.

We need not pursue the details of Kant's arguments beyond saying that Kant believed mathematical (and in particular geometrical) theorems to be examples of synthetic *a priori* judgements. Inasmuch as theorems are derived by a strict process of logical deduction from undeniable truths such as 'the whole is greater than any of its parts' they are true *a priori*. Kant believed them to be synthetic because mathematics does not analyse concepts, but rather *constructs* them. (The similarity of this view to that of Piaget – see Chapter 10 – will be obvious.)

How does Kant deal with the general problem of our knowledge of natural laws? He argues that: '*the understanding does not draw its laws* (a priori) *from nature, but prescribes them to nature*'. By this he means 'that laws which we discover in objects of sensible intuition, especially when they are recognised as necessary, are already held by us to be laws that the understanding has placed in them'. In

[1] Manchester University Press (1953), Ed. P. G. Lucas.

direct opposition to the empiricists, who argued that the human understanding is empty at birth and that it develops as a result of experience, Kant argues that 'the understanding is the origin of the universal order of nature'. (These quotations are from the *Prolegomena*.)

We cannot deal here with the details of Kant's arguments or with the criticisms that have been raised, particularly against his conception of the nature of mathematics. The most accessible treatment of this aspect of Kant's work is by A. J. Ayer: for a more technical criticism of Kant's philosophy the reader is referred to Bennett.[1]

Having briefly examined the foundations of empiricism and rationalism we shall now see how these ideas are relevant to present-day psychology, in particular the psychology of language. We can do little more than mention some of the important figures in this regard.

In his *Observations on Man* (1749)[2] David Hartley applied Locke's ideas to the construction of what would today be called physiological psychology. With his ideas of vibrations of nerves and their influence upon each other Hartley's thesis strikingly resembles that of Hebb's *The Organization of Behaviour* published exactly two hundred years later. The empiricists and Hartley were attacked by the 'commonsense' school of Scottish philosophers, including Reid (1710–96) who rejected empiricism on the grounds that it lowered the dignity of man, which is very much the objection that Koch raises against present-day behaviourism (Koch, 1964, etc.).

In the nineteenth century the mantle of the empiricists fell upon James Mill (1773–1836) and his son John Stuart Mill (1806–73). Both thinkers in their different ways attempted the contruction of a psychology based upon the association of ideas. It is interesting in the present context that Flugel in 1933 could write that 'Watson may perhaps be looked upon as the twentieth-century representative of the position occupied in the nineteenth century by James Mill'; whilst Mischel in 1968 argues that Hull's concept of increment of 'habit strength' (see Chapter 7) is equivalent to Mill's 'strength of association between ideas'. The details of the arguments need not concern us: the important point is that behaviourism can be seen to be in direct line of descent from the British Empiricists (for a discussion of the importance of Watson, see Bergmann).

[1] The reader wishing to know more about the philosophers discussed is referred to the following non-specialist accounts in addition to the references in the text: O'Connor (for Locke); Warnock (for Berkeley); Flew, Kemp Smith (for Hume); Körner (for Kant).
[2] For selections see Mandler and Mandler.

The two major representatives of rationalism in psychology today are Piaget and Chomsky, neither of whom is by original training a psychologist (Piaget being a biologist and Chomsky a linguist). Piaget's work is strikingly Kantian, with its investigations of the concepts of time, space, causality, the mechanisms of perception, and so on. The view is gradually being accepted that the solution of some of the major disputes of epistemology, particularly the nature of concepts, cannot be achieved without reference to psychological data: this point is argued by both Toulmin and Mischel in their contributions to Mischel's symposium on *Human Action*. This case has been argued explicitly by Piaget for the past twenty years, and the view has informed all his work for more than forty, but Mischel and Toulmin do not base their arguments on Piaget's work.

To appreciate Chomsky's position we must sketch the history of ideas in linguistics in the nineteenth century, basing this outline on the account given by Blumenthal. Then as now there were controversies between those scholars who preferred an empiricist account of language, emphasising description of observed linguistic usage, and others who followed the line of rationalism, or 'idealism' as it is often called in this connection (not to be confused with the 'subjective idealism' of Berkeley). The founder of the idealist tradition in linguistics was Wilhelm von Humboldt who in the early 1800s took the view that language was an *activity*, and one should be able to describe this activity by reference to a finite set of principles generating an infinite variety of speech. This school was much concerned with the subject-predicate structure of sentences, which was still a point of discussion until very recently (see Chapter 4).

A new empiricist group developed in the 1870s in opposition to von Humboldt's school. These *Junggrammatiker* (which is usually translated as 'neogrammarians', but in fact means 'young' grammarians, which is how they were contemptuously designated by the establishment – argument by pejorative epithet has a long history in linguistics) laid stress upon data collection and upon the study of languages according to the principles of physical science. The best-known representative of this school in the twentieth century was Ferdinand de Saussure, who in fact extended the school's horizons.

The relationship of the study of language to psychology was investigated by the *Junggrammatiker* under the influence of Herbart, who attempted to describe mental life mathematically. This relationship was further studied by Steinthal and Lazarus who in 1860 founded the *Zeitschrift für Völkerpsychologie und Sprachwissenschaft* (*Journal of social psychology and linguistics*). Steinthal argued that a science of language was a necessary part of a science of psychology, as it was through the innate laws of language and not through the senses that one gained primary access to the mind.

In 1875 Wundt was appointed to a chair of psychology at Leipzig. Wundt is generally remembered today for his studies of the content of sensations, but in fact carried out a great deal of work in what today would be called psycholinguistics. Blumenthal reminds us that Bloomfield (*Language,* 1933) regarded Wundt's work as the culmination of the nineteenth-century linguistic tradition begun by von Humboldt. According to Blumenthal it is this same tradition that has been renewed by Chomsky and his colleagues.

Chomsky's rationalism leads him to speculate that in 'the future, I think it not unlikely that the dogmatic character of the general empiricist framework and its inadequacy to human and animal intelligence will gradually become more evident' (Chomsky, 1968). This argument appears to overlook the dual nature of scientific progress, which requires two sorts of statement: heuristic statements and formal statements. The rationalist approach is ideal for formulating the heuristic statements that elucidate the nature of the problems facing us, but as we hope that we have made clear by a number of arguments in this chapter and the last, it is not so suitable for making these problems precise in a way that fits them for empirical demonstration. To eschew empirical demonstration leaves the problems in the realm of philosophical speculation from which science has sought to retrieve them. Conversely the empirical approach is fitted for the task of making precise, formal statements about scientific problems but not for formulating new problems requiring broad analysis. McKellar discusses these two approaches with regard to thinking; Beth and Piaget discuss them in respect of mathematics. It seems that, in science generally, both approaches are necessary, each modifying the other by their continual interplay.

Hume's empiricism awoke Kant from his intellectual slumbers and inspired him to found modern rationalism. Skinner's empiricism arouses both Chomsky and Koch to furies of denunciation, although it is not clear that contemporary rationalism has had the same order of success as contemporary empiricism. In the strange atmosphere of intolerance that pervades much of the writing of contemporary linguists and other anti-behaviourists one looks in vain for the respect that Kant showed for Hume. We may hope that the future will show less hostility and a greater awareness by both schools of their mutual dependence.

15

RETROSPECT AND PROSPECT

In the first chapter of this book we referred to Susanne Langer's *Philosophy in a New Key*. The new key referred to is one in which the importance in human affairs of the power of symbolisation is given due recognition. Langer argues that 'the importance of symbol-using, once admitted, soon becomes paramount in the study of intelligence' and furthermore that 'there is an increasing rap-prochement between philology and psychology – between the science of language and the science of what we do with language'.

Much of the present book has been written in Langer's new key, although the modulations through many variations may have de-parted from the home key signature. We have taken note of two approaches that adopt as a central theme the importance of the transformation of experience, which Langer identifies as the central human ability. These approaches are those of Piaget, who sees the development of the intellect as proceeding through a series of trans-formations made possible by the mechanism of reflective abstraction: and of Chomsky, who regards language as an inherent feature of the mind, and who views the use of language as embody-ing transformational rules whereby we make our meanings manifest.

We have paid attention to the dispute between contemporary psychological rationalism (as represented by Piaget and Chomsky) and contemporary psychological empiricism (as represented by the behaviourists). Essentially the dispute is between those who regard human acts as the product of symbolic transformations, and who therefore seek the origin of symbolisation; and those who treat behaviour and language as composed of acts existing in their own right. We have argued that the former approach has great heuristic power, whereas the second is better suited to formalisation of knowledge, and that scientific advance requires both. However, to argue in this way implies that the pioneering steps will be made by rationalism, the consolidation by empiricism. This implication we believe to be correct.

What of the future? We may expect to see the study of cognition playing an ever-increasing role in psychology. Taft, summarising the symposium in honour of Martin Scheerer (edited by Constance Scheerer), cites Scheerer as saying 'that the task in studying cognition is to discover the processes which underlie it, to determine the conditions for its occurence and its function in behaviour'. This formulation is clearly in the rationalist tradition. Chomsky believes that the study of language has much to contribute. He says '. . . the study of language may very well . . . provide a remarkably favourable perspective for the study of human mental processes. . . . It seems to me . . . that the study of language should occupy a central place in general psychology' (Chomsky, 1968, p. 84).

One promise that the future probably does not hold is an explanation of man's possession of language. We suggested in Chapter 13 that it would be helpful to accept that man is a language-using creature as a fact of natural life, and then to seek to characterise this language usage. Any characterisation must reflect the knowledge and beliefs current at the time the characterisation is made: this being so it follows that man's view of his own possession of language must be one of the perennial problems of metaphysics that require restating in each generation.

Chomsky quotes C. S. Peirce as saying that 'certain uniformities . . . prevail throughout the universe, and the reasoning mind is itself a product of this universe. These same laws are thus, by logical necessity, incorporated in its own being'. Chomsky finds 'Peirce's argument . . . entirely without force' (Chomsky, 1968, p. 82) but here we disagree. Peirce's argument finds its contemporary expression in the work of Piaget which, for all its flaws, probably offers a more consistent and comprehensive attempt to give an account of man in relation to his environment than any other at the present time. The influence of Piaget is only beginning to make itself felt in psychology, particularly in America, where few psychologists working in the field of general psychology ever refer to Piaget's investigations and theories. However, the situation is changing, and the accounts of Piaget's work by Baldwin, Flavell, and H. W. Maier in the USA, and various authors in Britain, may make Piaget's views as familiar as they deserve to be. Piaget may be wrong in many respects, but his writings probably contain more grains of truth than the works of the psychological polemicists whose work attracts so much attention these days. Given the right culture those grains could germinate to a rich harvest to nourish future generations of psychologists.

BIBLIOGRAPHY

Adorno, T. W., Frenkel-Brunswik, E., Levinson, N. and Sanford, R. N. (1950). *The Authoritarian Personality*. New York.

Anderson, H. H., Ed. (1959). *Creativity and Its Cultivation*. New York.

Austin, J. L. (1961). The meaning of a word. In *Philosophical Papers of the Late J. L. Austin*, Eds. Urmson, J. O., and Warnock, G. J. London.

Ayer, A. J. (1946). *Language, Truth and Logic*, 2nd ed. London.

Baldwin, A. L. (1967). *Theories of Child Development*. London.

Barber, C. (1965). *The Flux of Language*. London.

Barron, F. (1968). *Creativity and Personal Freedom*. London.

Bartlett, F. C. (1958). *Thinking: An Experimental and Social Study*. London.

Bay, E. (1969). The Lordat case and its import on the theory of aphasia. *Cortex*, **5**, 302–308.

Beard, R. M. (1969). *An Outline of Piaget's Developmental Psychology for Students and Teachers*. London.

Beekman, F. (1945). A celebrated case of cerebral injury. *Bulletin of the History of Medicine*, **17**, 521–526.

Beers, C. W. (1921). *A Mind that Found Itself*, 6th ed. New York.

Bennett, J. (1966). *Kant's Analytic*. Cambridge.

Bergmann, G. (1956). The contribution of John B. Watson. *Psychological Review*, **63**, 265–276 (reprinted in Saporta).

Berko, J. (1958). The child's learning of English morphology. *Word*, **14**, 150–177 (see also Berko and Brown).

Berko, J., and Brown, R. (1960). Psycholinguistic Research Methods. In *Handbook of Research Methods in Child Development*, Ed. Mussen, P. H. New York.

Bernstein, B. (1961a). Aspects of language and learning in the genesis of the social process. *Journal of Child Psychology and Psychiatry*, **1**, 313–324 (reprinted in Hymes).

Bernstein, B. (1961b). Social structure, language, and learning. *Educational Research*, **3**, 163–176 (reprinted in De Cecco).

Beth, E. W., and Piaget, J. (1966). *Mathematical Epistemology and Psychology*. Dordrecht, Holland.

Bett, H. (1936). *Wanderings among Words*. London.

Blanc, A. C. (1962). Some Evidence for the Ideologies of Early Man. In *The Social Life of Early Man*, Ed. Washburn, S. London.

Blumenthal, A. L., Ed. (1970). *Language and Psychology: Historical Aspects of Psycholinguistics*. London.

Boas, G. (1966). *The Cult of Childhood*. London.

Bodmer, F. (1943). *The Loom of Language: A Guide to Foreign Languages for the Home Student*. London.

Bolinger, D. (1968). *Aspects of Language*. New York.

Boring, E. G. (1950a). *A History of Experimental Psychology*, 2nd ed. New York.

Boring, E. G. (1950b). Great men and scientific progress. *Proceedings of the American Philosophical Society*, **94**, 339–351 reprinted in *History, Psychology, and Science: Selected Papers by Edwin G. Boring*, Eds. Watson, R. I., and Campbell, D. T. 1963. London.

Bourne, L. E. (1966). *Human Conceptual Behaviour*. Boston.

Boyle, D. G. (1969). *A Students' Guide to Piaget*. Oxford.

Brearley, M., and Hitchfield, E. (1966). *A Teacher's Guide to Reading Piaget*. London.

Broadbent, D. E. (1958). *Perception and Communication*. Oxford.

Broadbent, D. E. (1961). *Behaviour*. London.

Broadbent, D. E. (1970). In defence of empirical psychology. *Bulletin of the British Psychological Society*, **23**, 87–96 (for a reply to this paper see Cromer).

Bruner, J. S. (1964). The course of cognitive growth. *American Psychologist*, **19**, 1–15 (reprinted in Jones and in Wason and Johnson-Laird).

Bruner, J. S., Goodnow, J. J., and Austin G. A. (1956). *A Study of Thinking*. London.

Bruner, J. S., Olver, R. R., and Greenfield, P. M. *et al.* (1966). *Studies in Cognitive Growth*. London.

Brunswik, E. (1956). *Perception and the Representative Design of Psychological Experiments*. Berkeley.

Burt, C. (1962). The psychology of creativity (a critical notice of *Creativity and Intelligence* by Getzels, J. W., and Jackson, P. W.). *British Journal of Educational Psychology*, **32**, 292–298.

Burt C. (1967). The genetic determination of intelligence: a reply. *British Journal of Psychology*, **58**, 153–162 (actually published in 1968).

Burt, C. (1968). Mental capacity and its critics. *Bulletin of the British Psychological Society*, **21**, 11–18.

Caillois, R. (1962). *Man, Play, and Games*. London (from the French *Les Jeux et les Hommes*, 1958).

Campbell, D. T. (1968). A Phenomenology of the Other One: Corrigible, Hypothetical and Critical. In Mischel.

Carnap, R. (1937). *The Logical Syntax of Language*. London.

Carroll, J. B. (1960). Language Development in Children. In *Encyclopaedia of Educational Research*. London (reprinted in Saporta).

Carroll, J. B. (1964a). *Language and Thought*. Englewood Cliffs, N.J.

Carroll, J. B. (1964b). Words, meanings and concepts. *Harvard Educational Review*, 34, 178–202 (reprinted in Jakovobits and Miron).

Castiglioni, A. (1946). *Adventures of the Mind*. London.

Chase, R. A. (1966). Evolutionary Aspects of Language Development and Function: A Discussion of Lenneberg's Presentation (see Lenneberg, 1966). In Smith and Miller.

Cherry, C. (1966). *On Human Communication: A Review, a Survey, and a Criticism*, 2nd ed. London.

Chomsky, N. (1957). *Syntactic Structures*. The Hague.

Chomsky, N. (1959). Review of *Verbal Behaviour* by Skinner, B. F. *Language*, 35, 26–58 (reprinted in abridged form in De Cecco).

Chomsky, N. (1968). *Language and Mind*. New York.

Cole, M. (1968). The anatomical basis of aphasia as seen by Pierre Marie. *Cortex*, 4, 172–183.

Cowles, J. T. (1937). Food-tokens as incentives for learning by chimpanzees. *Comparative Psychology Monographs*, 14, no. 5.

Crafts, L. W., Schneirla, T. C., Robinson, E. E., and Gilbert, R. W. (1950). *Recent Experiments in Psychology*. London.

Cromer, R. F. (1970). In defence of empirical method: a reply to Broadbent concerning psycholinguistics. *Bulletin of the British Psychological Society*, 23, 271–279.

De Bono E. (1970). *Lateral Thinking: A Textbook of Creativity*. London (chapter 20 – The New Word Po – is available separately).

De Cecco, J. P., Ed. (1967). *The Psychology of Language, Thought and Instruction: Readings*. London.

De Saussure, F. (1959). *Course in General Linguistics*. New York (original French ed. 1916).

Duncan, C. P., Ed. (1967). *Thinking: Current Experimental Studies*. New York.

Duncker, K. (1945). On problem solving. *Psychological Monographs*, 58, no. 5 (original German ed. 1935).

Evans, B. (1946). *The Natural History of Nonsense*. New York.

Feigl, H. (1960). Mind-Body, *Not* a Pseudo-Problem. In *Dimensions of Mind*, Ed. Hook S. New York (reprinted in Scher).

Flavell, J. H. (1963). *The Developmental Psychology of Jean Piaget*. London.

Fletcher, R. (1968). *Instinct in Man in the Light of Recent Work in Comparative Psychology*. 2nd ed. London.

Flew, A. (1962). *David Hume on Human Nature and the Understanding: Edited with an Introduction and an Annotated Index*. London.

Flugel, J. C. (revised West, D. J. 1964). *A Hundred Years of Psychology*. London.

Fodor, J. A. (1965). Could meaning be an r_m? *Journal of Verbal Learning and Verbal Behaviour*, 4, 73–81 (reprinted in Oldfield and Marshall).

Foulkes, D. (1966). *The Psychology of Sleep*. New York.

Freeman, J., Butcher, H. J., and Christie, T. (1968). *Creativity: A Selective Review of Research*. London.

Freud, S. (1953). *The Interpretation of Dreams*. London (original German ed. 1900).

Frisch, K. von (1955). *The Dancing Bees: An Account of the Life and Senses of the Honey Bee*. New York.

Fromm, E. (1952). *The Forgotten Language: An Introduction to the Understanding of Dreams, Fairy Tales, and Myths*. London.

Furth, H. G. (1966). *Thinking Without Language: Psychological Implications of Deafness*. London.

Galton, F. (1883). *Inquiries into Human Faculty and its Development*. London.

Gazzaniga, M. S. (1967). The split brain in man. *Scientific American*, **217**, 24–29.

Gellner, E. (1959). *Words and Things: A Critical Account of Linguistic Philosophy and a Study in Ideology*. London.

Geschwind, N., and Fusillo, M. (1966). Colour-naming defects in association with alexia. *Archives of Neurology*, **15**, 137–146.

Gesell, A. L. (1941). *Wolf Child and Human Child: Being a Narrative Interpretation of the Life History of Kamala, the Wolf Girl*. London.

Getzels, J. W., and Jackson, P. W. (1962). *Creativity and Intelligence: Explorations with Gifted Children*. London.

Ghiselin, B., Ed. (1952). *The Creative Process: A Symposium*. New York.

Goad, H. (1958). *Language in History*. London.

Goldstein, K. (1948). *Language and Language Disturbances: Aphasic Symptom Complexes and their Significance for Medicine and Theory of Language*. New York.

Gombrich, E. H. (1960). *Art and Illusion: A Study in the Psychology of Pictorial Representation*. London.

Gombrich, E. H. (1963). *Meditations on a Hobby Horse: And Other Essays on the Theory of Art*. London.

Guilford, J. P. (1967). *The Nature of Intelligence*. London.

Hampshire, S. (1960). *Thought and Action*. London.

Haugen, E. (1956). The Bilingual Individual. In *Bilingualism in the Americas: A Bibliography and Research Guide* by Haugen, E. American Dialect Society Publication no. 26. Alabama (reprinted in Saporta).

Hayes, C. (1951). *The Ape in Our House*. New York.

Head, H. (1926). *Aphasia and Kindred Disorders of Speech*. Cambridge.

Hebb, D. O. (1949). *The Organization of Behaviour: A Neuropsychological Theory*. London.

Hebb, D. O. (1955). Drives and the CNS (conceptual nervous system). *Psychological Review*, **62**, 243–254.

Heidbreder, E. (1946, 1947, 1948, 1949). The attainment of concepts. In *Journal of General Psychology*, **35**, 173–223; *Journal of Psychology*, **24**, 93–138; ibid., **25**, 299–329; ibid., **26**, 45–69 and 193–216; ibid., **27**, 3–39 and 263–309.

Henschen, F. (1966). *The Human Skull: A Cultural History.* London.

Herriot, P. (1970). *An Introduction to the Psychology of Language.* London.

Hockett, C. F. (1960). The origin of speech. *Scientific American,* **203,** 89–96.

Holz, W. C., and Azrin, N. H. (1966). Conditioning Human Verbal Behaviour. In *Operant Behaviour,* Ed. Honig, W. K. New York.

Hudson, L. (1966). *Contrary Imaginations: A Psychological Study of the English Schoolboy.* London.

Huizinga, J. (1949). *Homo Ludens: A Study of the Play Elements in Culture.* London. (ch. 12 reprinted in Larrabee and Meyersohn).

Hull, C. L. (1943). *Principles of Behaviour: An Introduction to Behaviour Theory.* New York (see Broadbent, 1961, for full references).

Hymes, D., Ed. (1964). *Language in Culture and Society: A Reader in Linguistics and Anthropology.* London.

Inhelder, B., Bovet, M., and Smock, C. D. (1966). On cognitive development. *American Psychologist,* **21,** 160–164.

Itard, E. M. (1962). *The Wild Boy of Aveyron.* New York (original French ed. 1802).

Jackson, J. H. (1932). Notes on the Physiology of the Nervous System. In *Selected Writings of Hughlings Jackson,* Ed. Taylor, J., vol. 2. London.

Jacobsen, L. E. (1932). The electrophysiology of mental activities. *American Journal of Psychology,* **44,** 677–694.

Jaensch, E. R. (see Klüver).

Jakobovits, L. A., and Miron, M. S., Eds. (1967). *Readings in the Psychology of Language.* London.

Jakobson, R. (1955). Aphasia as a Linguistic Problem. In *On Expressive Language,* Ed. Werner, H. Worcester, Mass. (reprinted in Saporta).

Jones, R. M., Ed. (1966). *Contemporary Educational Psychology: Selected Readings.* London.

Katz, J. J., and Fodor, J. A. (1963). The structure of a semantic theory. *Language,* **39,** 170–210 (reprinted in abridged form in De Cecco; and in full in Jakobovits and Miron).

Keeling, S. V. (1968). *Descartes,* 2nd ed. London.

Kellogg, W. N., and Kellogg, L. A. (1933). *The Ape and the Child: A Study of Environmental Influence upon Early Behaviour.* London.

Kelly, G. A. (1955). *The Psychology of Personal Constructs.* New York.

Kemp Smith, N. (1941). *The Philosophy of David Hume: A Critical Study of Its Origins and Central Doctrines.* London.

Kline, M. (1963). *Mathematics in Western Culture.* New York.

Klüver, H. (1928). Studies on the eidetic type and on eidetic imagery. *Psychological Bulletin,* **25,** 69–104 (includes a full account of Jaensch's work).

Koch, S., Ed. (1959–63, continuing). *Psychology: the Study of a Science.* London.

Koch, S. (1964). Psychology and Emerging Conceptions of Knowledge as Unitary. In Wann (Ed.).

Koestler, A. (1964). *The Act of Creation.* London.

Koestler, A. (1967). *The Ghost in the Machine*. London.

Köhler, W. (1925). *The Mentality of Apes*. London.

Körner, S. (1955). *Kant*. London.

Krechevsky, I. (1932). 'Hypotheses' in rats. *Psychological Review*, **39**, 516–532.

Kubie, L. S. (1954). The forgotten man of education. *Harvard Alumni Bulletin*, **56**, 349–353 (this and another paper by Kubie are reprinted in Jones).

Laing, R. D. (1967). *The Politics of Experience and The Bird of Paradise*. London.

Lambert, W. E., and Fillenbaum, S. (1959). A pilot study of aphasia among bilinguals. *Canadian Journal of Psychology*, **13**, 28–34 (reprinted in Saporta).

Landar, H. (1966). *Language and Culture*. London.

Langer, S. K. (1951). *Philosophy in a New Key: A Study in the Symbolism of Reason, Rite and Art*. 2nd ed. London.

Larrabee, E., and Meyersohn, R., Eds. (1958). *Mass Leisure*. Glencoe, Illinois.

Lashley, K. S. (1929). *Brain Mechanisms and Intelligence*. Chicago.

Lashley, K. S. (1951). The Problem of Serial Order in Behaviour. In *Cerebral Mechanisms in Behaviour*, Ed. Jeffress, L. A. (reprinted in Saporta).

Lenneberg, E. H. (1960). Review of *Speech and Brain Mechanisms* by Penfield, W., and Roberts, L. *Language*, **36**, 97–112. (reprinted in Oldfield and Marshall).

Lenneberg, E. H. (1966). The Natural History of Language. In Smith and Miller.

Lenneberg, E. H. (1967). *Biological Foundations of Language*. With appendices by Noam Chomsky and Otto Marx. London.

Luchins, A. S. (1942). Mechanization in problem-solving. *Psychological Monographs*, **54**, 1–95.

Luchins, A. S., and Luchins, E. H. (1950). New experimental attempts at preventing mechanization in problem-solving. *Journal of General Psychology*, **42**, 279–297.

Luria, A. R. (1959). The directive function of speech in development and dissolution. Pt. I, *Word*, **15**, 341–352; Pt. II, *Word*, **15**, 453–464 (reprinted in Oldfield and Marshall).

Luria, A. R. (1961). *The Role of Speech in the Regulation of Normal and Abnormal Behaviour*. Oxford.

Luria, A. R. (1969). *The Origin and Cerebral Organization of Man's Conscious Action*. Moscow.

McCarthy, D. (1954). Language Development in Children. In *Manual of Child Psychology*, 2nd ed. Ed. Carmichael, L. London (3rd ed., Ed. McNeill, 1970).

MacCorquodale, K. (1970). On Chomsky's review of Skinner's *Verbal Behaviour*. *Journal of the Experimental Analysis of Behaviour*, **13**, 83–99.

McKellar, P. (1957). *Imagination and Thinking*. London.

McLuhan, M. (1968). *McLuhan Hot and Cold*. London.

Maier, H. W. (1965). *Three Theories of Child Development: The Contributions of Erik H. Erikson, Jean Piaget, and Robert R. Sears and Their Applications*. London.

Maier, N. R. F. (1929). Reasoning in white rats. *Comparative Psychology Monographs*, **6**, no. 3.

Maier, N. R. F. (1930, 1931). Reasoning in humans. I: On direction, *Journal of Comparative Psychology*, **10**, 115–114; II: The solution of a problem and its appearance in consciousness, ibid., **12**, 181–194.

Maier, N. R. F. (1933). An aspect of human reasoning. *British Journal of Psychology*, **24**, 144–155.

Maltzman, I. (1955). Thinking: from a behaviourist point of view. *Psychological Review*, **62**, 275–286 (reprinted in De Cecco and in Duncan).

Mandler, J. M., and Mandler, G., Eds. (1964). *Thinking: From Association to Gestalt*. London.

Marx, O. M. (1966). Aphasia studies and language theory in the nineteenth century. *Bulletin of the History of Medicine*, **40**, 328–349.

Max, L. W. (1935). An experimental study of the motor theory of consciousness. III: Action current responses in deaf-mutes during sleep, sensory stimulation and dreams, *Journal of Comparative Psychology*, **19**, 469–486; IV: Action current responses in the deaf during, awakening, kinaesthetic imagery and abstract thinking, ibid., **24**, 301–344.

Millar, S. (1968). *The Psychology of Play*. London.

Miller, G. A. (1951). *Language and Communication*. London.

Miller, G. A. (1965). Some preliminaries to psycholinguistics. *American Psychologist*, **20**, 15–20 (reprinted in De Cecco, Jakobovits and Miron, and Oldfield and Marshall).

Miller, G. A., Galanter, E., and Pribram, K. L. (1960). *Plans and the Structure of Behaviour*. London.

Miller, G. A., and Selfridge, J. A. (1953). Verbal context and the recall of meaningful material. *American Journal of Psychology*, **63**, 176–185 (reprinted in Saporta).

Mischel, T. (1968). Scientific and Philosophical Psychology: A Historical Introduction. In Mischel (Ed.). See following reference.

Mischel, T., Ed. (1968). *Human Action: Conceptual and Empirical Issues*. London.

Moore, G. E. (1936). Is existence a predicate? *Supplementary Proceedings of the Aristotelian Society*, **36**, 175–188.

Moreno, J. L. (1953). *Who Shall Survive? Foundations of Sociometry Group Psychotherapy and Sociodrama*, 2nd ed. New York.

Morris, C. W. (1938). *Foundations of the Theory of Signs*. Chicago (vol. 1, no. 5, of the International Encyclopaedia of Unified Science).

Morris, C. W. (1946). *Signs, Language and Behaviour*. London.

Moruzzi, G., and Magoun, H. W. (1949). Brainstem reticular formation and activation of EEG. *EEG and Clinical Neurophysiology*, 1, 455–473.

Mowrer, O. H. (1950). *Learning Theory and Personality Dynamics*. New York.

Mowrer, O. H. (1954). The psychologist looks at language. *American Psychologist*, 9, 660–694 (reprinted in Jakobovits and Miron).

Mowrer, O. H. (1960). *Learning Theory and the Symbolic Process*. London.

Mowrer, O. H. (1961). *The Crisis in Psychiatry and Religion*. London.

Neisser, U. (1963). The multiplicity of thought. *British Journal of Psychology*, 54, 1–14 (reprinted in Jones).

Newell, A., Shaw, J. C., and Simon, H. A. (1962). The Processes of Creative Thinking. In *Contemporary Approaches to Creative Thinking: A Symposium*, Eds. Gruber, H. E., Terrell, G., and Wertheimer, Michael. New York.

Newton-de Molina, D. (1969). George Steiner's *Language and Silence*. *Critical Quarterly*, 11, 365–374.

Newton-de Molina, D. (1970). McLuhan: ice cold. *Critical Quarterly*, 12, 78–88.

O'Connor, D. J. (1952). *John Locke*. London.

Ogden, C. K., and Richards, I. A. (1953). *The Meaning of Meaning: A Study of the Influence of Language upon Thought and of the Science of Symbolism*, 8th ed. London.

Oldfield, R. C., and Marshall, J. C., Eds. (1968). *Language: Selected Readings*. London.

Osgood, C. E. (1953). *Method and Theory in Experimental Psychology*. London.

Osgood, C. E., Suci, G., and Tannenbaum, P. (1957). *The Measurement of Meaning*. Urbana, Illinois.

Pei, M. (1962). *Voices of Man: the Meaning and Function of Language*. London.

Pei, M. (1966). *The Story of Language,* 2nd ed. London.

Peirce, C. S. (1931–58). *Collected Papers* (8 vols.). London.

Penfield, W. S., and Roberts, L. (1959). *Speech and Brain Mechanisms*. Princeton.

Piaget, J. (1950). *Introduction à l'Épistémologie Génétique*. Paris.

Piaget, J. (1951). *Play, Dreams and Imitation in Childhood*. London.

Piaget, J. (1959). *The Language and Thought of the Child*, 2nd ed. London.

Piaget, J. (1961). The genetic approach to the psychology of thought. *Journal of Educational Psychology*, 52, 275–281 (reprinted in De Cecco and in Stones).

Piaget, J. (1970). *Genetic Epistemology*. London.

Piaget, J., and Inhelder, B. (1969). *The Psychology of the Child*. London.

Pitcher, G. (1964). *The Philosophy of Wittgenstein*. London.

Potter, S. (1950). *Our Language*. Harmondsworth. London.

Pratt, C. C. (1950). The role of past experience in visual perception. *Journal of Psychology*, 30, 85–107.

Premack, D. (1970). A functional analysis of language. *Journal of the Experimental Analysis of Behaviour*, 14, 107–125.

Ray, W. S. (1967). *The Experimental Psychology of Original Thinking*. London.

Richardson, A. (1969). *Mental Imagery*. London.

Richmond, W. K. (1963). *Culture and General Education*. London.

Riese, W. (1947). The early history of aphasia. *Bulletin of the History of Medicine*, 21, 322–334.

Riese, W. (1954). Auto-observation of aphasia: reported by an eminent nineteenth century medical scientist. *Bulletin of the History of Medicine*, 28, 237–243.

Riopelle, A. J., Ed. (1967). *Animal Problem Solving*. London.

Rokeach, M. (1960). *The Open and Closed Mind: Investigations into the Nature of Belief Systems and Personality Systems*. New York.

Rugg, H. (1963). *Imagination: An Inquiry into the Sources and Conditions that Stimulate Creativity*. London.

Ryle, G. (1949). *The Concept of Mind*. London.

Sapir, E. (1921). *Language: An Introduction to the Study of Speech*. New York.

Sapir, E. (1933). Language. *Encyclopaedia of the Social Sciences*. London.

Saporta, S., Ed. (1961). *Psycholinguistics: A Book of Readings*. London.

Sarno, J. E., Swisher, L. P., and Sarno, M. T. (1969). Aphasia in a congenitally deaf man. *Cortex*, 5, 398–414.

Scheerer, C., Ed. (1964). *Cognition: Theory, Research, Promise*. London.

Scher, J., Ed. (1962). *Theories of the Mind*. Glencoe, Illinois.

Schiller, C. H., Trans. and Ed. (1957). *Instinctive Behaviour: The Development of a Modern Concept*. New York.

Schlosberg, H. (1947). The concept of play. *Psychological Review*, 54, 229–231.

Schrödinger, E. (1944). *What Is Life? The Physical Aspect of the Living Cell*. Cambridge.

Schuell, H., and Jenkins, J. J. (1959). The nature of language deficit in aphasia. *Psychological Review*, 66, 45–67 (reprinted in Saporta).

Shannon, C. E. (1948). *A Mathematical Theory of Communication*. Bell Telephone System Monograph B-1598.

Skinner, B. F. (1938). *The Behaviour of Organisms: An Experimental Analysis*. New York.

Skinner, B. F. (1957). *Verbal Behaviour*. New York.

Smith, F., and Miller, G. A., Eds. (1966). *The Genesis of Language: A Psycholinguistic Approach*. London.

Smith, S. M., Brown, H. O., Toman, J. E. P., and Goodman, L. S. (1947). The lack of cerebral effects of d-tubocurarine. *Anaesthesiology*, 8, 1–14.

Snaith, W. (1965). *The Irresponsible Arts*. London.

Sperry, R. W. (1964). The great cerebral commisure. *Scientific American*, 210, 42–52.

Spier, L., Hallowell, A. I., and Newman, S. S., Eds. (1941). *Language, Culture and Personality: Essays in Memory of Edward Sapir*. Menasha, Wisconsin.

Steiner, G. (1967). *Language and Silence, Essays 1958–1966*. London.

Stones, E. (1970). *Readings in Educational Psychology: Learning and Teaching*. London.

Strawson, P. F. (1962). *Introduction to Logical Theory*. London.

Taylor, C. W., Ed. (1964a). *Creativity: Progress and Potential*. London.

Taylor, C. W., Ed. (1964b). *Widening Horizons in Creativity: The Proceedings of the Fifth Utah Creativity Research Conference*. London.

Taylor, C. W., and Williams, F. E., Eds. (1966). *Instructional Media and Creativity: The Proceedings of the Sixth Utah Creativity Research Conference*. London.

Temkin, O. (1947). Gall and the phrenological movement. *Bulletin of the History of Medicine*, **21**, 275–321.

Thorpe, W. H. (1956). *Learning and Instinct in Animals*. London.

Tolman, E. C. (1932). *Purposive Behaviour in Animals and Men*. New York (see Broadbent, 1961, for full references).

Toulmin, S. (1961). *Foresight and Understanding: An Enquiry into the Aims of Science*. London.

Toulmin, S. (1968). Concepts and the Explanation of Behaviour. In Mischel (Ed.).

Treisman, A. M. (1964). The effect of irrelevant material on the efficiency of selective listening. *American Journal of Psychology*, **77**, 533–546 (reprinted in Oldfield and Marshall).

Vigotsky, L. S. (1962). *Thought and Language*. London (original Russian publication 1934).

Wagner, G. (1968). *On the Wisdom of Words*. London.

Wallach, M. A., and Kogan, N. (1965). *Modes of Thinking in Young Children: A Study of the Creativity – Intelligence Distinction*. London.

Wallas, G. (1926). *The Art of Thought*. London.

Wann, T. W., Ed. (1964). *Behaviourism and Phenomenology: Contrasting Bases for Modern Psychology*. London.

Warnock, G. (1953). *Berkeley*. Harmondsworth. London.

Wason, P. C., and Johnson-Laird, P. N., Eds. (1968). *Thinking and Reasoning: Selected Readings*. London.

Watson, J. B. (1920). Is thinking merely the action of the language mechanisms? *British Journal of Psychology*, **11**, 86–104.

Wechsler, D. (1958). *The Measurement and Appraisal of Adult Intelligence*, 4th ed. Baltimore.

Welch, L., and Long, L. (1940). The higher structural phases of concept formation in children. *Journal of Psychology*, **9**, 59–95.

Werner, H., and Kaplan, E. (1950). Development of word meaning through verbal context: an experimental study. *Journal of Psychology*, **29**, 251–257 (reprinted in De Cecco).

Wertheimer, M. (1950). The Syllogism and Productive Thinking. In *A Source Book of Gestalt Psychology*, Ed. Ellis, W. D. London (reprinted in Mandler and Mandler; original German publication 1920).

Wertheimer, M. (1959). *Productive Thinking*, 2nd ed. London.

White, R. J. (1970). *The Anti-Philosophers: A Study of the Philosophes in Eighteenth-Century France*. London.

Whorf, B. L. (1939). The Relation of Habitual Thought and Behaviour to Language. In Whorf (1956). See following reference (reprinted in Spier *et al.*).

Whorf, B. L. (1956). *Language, Thought, and Reality: Selected Writings of Benjamin Lee Whorf*, edited and with an introduction by Carroll, J. B. London.

Wilkie, J. S. (1953). *The Science of Mind and Brain*. London.

Witkin, H. A. (1949). Perception of body position and of the position of the visual field. *Psychological Monographs: General and Applied*, **63**, no. 302, 1–46.

Witkin, H. A., Lewis, H. B., Hertzman, K. Meissner, P. B., and Wapner, S. (1954). *Personality through Perception*. London.

Wittgenstein, L. (1953). *Philosophical Investigations*. Oxford.

Wolfe, J. B. (1936). Effectiveness of token-rewards for chimpanzees. *Comparative Psychology Monographs*, **12**, no. 5.

Wolfenstein, M. (1951). The emergence of fun morality. *Journal of Social Issues*, **7**, 15–25 (reprinted in Larrabee and Meyersohn).

Wolff, R. P. (1963). *Kant's Theory of Mental Activity*. Cambridge, Mass.

Woodworth, R. S., and Schlosberg, H. (1955). *Experimental Psychology*, 2nd ed. London.

Yerkes, R. M., and Yerkes, A. W. (1929). *The Great Apes*. London.

Zipf, G. K. (1949). *Human Behaviour and the Principle of Least Effort*. London.

In addition to the works listed above, which have been referred to in the text, the following have been consulted in the preparation of this book.

Henle, P., Ed. (1958). *Language, Thought and Culture*. Ann Arbor, Michigan.

Parry, J. (1967). *The Psychology of Human Communication*. London.

Terwilliger, R. F. (1968). *Meaning and Mind: A Study in the Psychology of Language*. London.

SUBJECT INDEX

NAME INDEX

ADORNO, T. W. (with others), 58, 171
Anderson, H. H., 97, 171
Annett, M., 128 n., 131 n.
Aristotle, 154, 155
Austin, J. L., 143, 171
Ayer, A. J., 43–4, 46, 119, 142–5, 164, 171

BALDWIN, A. L., 168, 171
Barber, C., 42, 171
Barron, F., 98, 171
Bartlett, F. C., 82–4, 86, 171
Bay, E., 135, 171
Beard, R. M., 124, 171
Beekman, F., 171
Beers, C. W., 52, 53, 171
Bennett, J., 164, 171
Bergmann, George, 164, 171
Berkeley, G., 64, 161–2, 165
Berko, J., 24, 171
Bernstein, B., 46–7, 171
Beth, E. W. (with J. Piaget), 39, 116, 157, 166, 172
Bett, H., 43, 172
Blanc, A. C., 59, 172
Bloomfield, L., 166
Blumenthal, A. L., 165, 172
Boas, G., 98, 99, 172
Bodmer, F., 41, 172

Bolinger, D., 36, 42, 172
Boring, E. G., 100, 172
Bourbaki, N., 119–20
Bourne, L. E., 110, 172
Boyle, D. G., 111, 118, 172
Brearley, M., 124, 172
Broadbent, D. E., 27, 28, 31, 61, 64, 172
Broca, P., 133
Brown, R., 24, 152, 171
Bruner, J. S., 24, 25, 111, 124, 172; (with Goodnow and Austin), 105, 107–10, 172; (with Olver, Greenfield et al), 111, 172
Brunswik, E., 38, 172
Burt, C., 85, 89, 172

CAILLOIS, R., 63, 172
Campbell, D. T., 64, 172
Cantor, G., 118
Carnap, R., 41, 172
Carroll, J. B., 24, 34, 104, 173, 181
Castiglioni, A., 54, 173
Chase, R. A., 153, 173
Cherry, C., 31, 33, 34, 35, 173
Chomsky, N., 26–8, 34, 35, 36, 61, 112, 119, 147, 155–6, 165–6, 167, 168, 173